educational technology in engineering

Prepared by

Lionel V. Baldwin and *Kenneth S. Down*
for the
National Academy of Engineering

NATIONAL ACADEMY PRESS

Washington, D.C. 1981

The National Academy of Engineering is a private organization
established in 1964 to share in the responsibility given the National
Academy of Sciences under its congressional charter of 1863 to
recognize distinguished engineers; to examine questions of science and
technology at the request of the federal government; to sponsor
engineering programs aimed at meeting national needs; and to encourage
engineering research.

Library of Congress Catalog Card Number 81-80333

International Standard Book Number 0-309-03138-9

Available from

NATIONAL ACADEMY PRESS
2101 Constitution Avenue, N.W.
Washington, D.C. 20418

Printed in the United States of America

FOREWORD

Since its founding, the National Academy of Engineering (NAE) has taken a major interest in engineering education. For several years there was a Council on Engineering Education which produced much work including an early report summarizing available educational films in the engineering area. Even though this document is out of print, we still receive occasional requests for it.

In 1978, the NAE formed an <u>ad hoc</u> committee on Advanced Technology in Engineering Education. At that time, an excellent treatise on educational technology in engineering was prepared by Dean Lionel V. Baldwin of Colorado State University and Associate Dean Kenneth S. Down of Stanford University. The obvious utility of this document led us to ask the authors to update the material in order that we could make it available to the many people interested in this important subject.

Courtland D. Perkins
President
National Academy of Engineering

PREFACE

This paper reviews the literature and current knowledge on the use
of modern technological methods in engineering education with an
emphasis on videotape systems. The primary focus is on current
practices. In the concluding two chapters, we make a critical
evaluation of today's activities and offer some recommendations for
future activities.

We do not attempt to summarize the many reports concerning
educational technology which offer rationale for government action. The
National Academy of Engineering is clearly addressing the correct
issue: how to improve the quality of engineering education.

No pretense is made that this report is complete, but we hope it
offers a representative sampling of good practice today. The authors
would welcome comments. The authors also would like to express their
appreciation to Linda L. Jenstrom for her editorial assistance in
preparing this manuscript.

Lionel V. Baldwin
Colorado State University

Kenneth S. Down
Stanford University

v

CONTENTS

LIST OF TABLES AND FIGURES

ABBREVIATIONS

ACE	Association for Continuing Education
ACS	American Chemical Society
AMCEE	Association for Media-Based Continuing Education for Engineers
ASEE	American Society for Engineering Education
BBC	British Broadcasting Company
CAD	computer-aided design
CAES-MIT	Center for Advanced Engineering Study, Massachusetts Institute of Technology
CAI	computer-assisted instruction
CAM	computer-aided manufacturing
CATV	cable (television) delivery systems
CMI	computer-managed instruction
CPA	Certified Public Accountant
CSU	Colorado State University
DISCUS	Disposal and Collection User Simulation
DOE	Department of Energy
ECPD/ABET	Engineer's Council for Professional Development/ Accreditation Board for Engineering and Technology
EIT	Engineer in Training
ET	educational technology
ETV	educational television
FCC	Federal Communications Commission
IEEE	Institute of Electrical and Electronics Engineers
ITFS	instructional television fixed service
ITV	instructional television
MIT	Massachusetts Institute of Technology
NAE	National Academy of Engineering
NASA	National Aeronautics and Space Administration
NIE	National Institute of Education
NPR	National Public Radio
NRC	National Research Council
NSF	National Science Foundation
PBS	Public Broadcasting Service
PLATO	Programmed Logic for Automatic Teaching Operations

PSI	personalized system of instruction
RIT	Rochester Institute of Technology
RPI	Rensselaer Polytechnic Institute
TICCIT	Time-shared Interactive Computer Controlled Information Television
TVI	tutored videotaped instruction
USC	University of Southern California

SUMMARY

Educational technology (ET) encompasses not only the use of
materials and hardware to aid in the learning process, but also the
systematic organization and presentation of knowledge to the learner.
The rejuvenated interest in ET today stems from the microelectronics
revolution of the past decade which, coupled with the development of
digital and laser systems, is just starting to produce useful
instructional hardware that is more powerful and more affordable.
Indeed, some items are intended for direct consumer purchase.

The challenge of devising appropriate ways to employ hardware in
education is stressed throughout this paper. Much of the text focuses
on effective examples of ET as it is practiced in engineering
education. The recommendations, presented after this summary, call for
new programs which would capitalize on the decentralization of the new,
inexpensive, stand-alone ET delivery systems.

Three major goals for introducing ET are: 1) to save dollars;
2) to enrich, improve, and individualize instruction; and 3) to serve
the unserved or enlarge coverage. By documenting the specific goals
and results of ET applications in the economic context of <u>productivity</u>,
educators could describe a wide array of goals for ET in terms readily
understood by those who make policy. Actual examples of courses are
used to illustrate the productivity concept; situations in which
additional outputs are identified that justify the additional input of
ET are described.

Instructional television (ITV) in engineering education on campus
is often not popular with undergraduates when it is substituted for
live lectures. Early ITV uses were viewed as too impersonal by many
students. Yet, through careful implementation, ITV can demonstrably
enhance learning, and, at the same time, lower the cost of
instruction. The first course in accounting at Colorado State
University is an excellent example. This course is built around 20- to
25-minute lectures which are studio produced, well illustrated, and
continually revised. Groups of approximately 30 students viewing a
brief ITV lecture are proctored by graduate teaching assistants.
Immediately afterwards, the assistants lead discussions and interactive
problem-solving sessions. In each of the past 14 years, over 500

students have been exposed to standardized content in relatively small classes at less than $1.50 per student-contact-hour. These students consistently score in the top 25th percentile of the national Certified Public Accountant (CPA) examination for Level I, beginning accounting. The key points that have made the course a success seem to be: simplicity of presentation and active participation by the students.

Today, many engineering faculties are faced with record numbers of students. Problems such as having to teach very large classes and having to turn away students are commonplace. Properly applied, ITV could be a cost-effective alternative, yet it languishes on most campuses. More efforts to achieve both effective and popular applications are required.

Included among the more popular applications is the instant replay of classroom lectures under the guidance of a tutor. Such a program is used by the Massachusetts Institute of Technology to stem the attrition of ethnic minority undergraduates. Lecture review by way of cable delivery systems (CATV) to dormitories and to library self-study carrels also is popular. Some experiments involving the use of videotape in self-paced instruction show promise.

Student performance in oral and written communication skills has been improved by audiotape and videotape experiences. Individual laboratory reports are critiqued by Southern Methodist University instructors using audio cassettes in a very personal, effective manner. The opportunity to view one's own presentation by videotape replay and to be coached by peers and teachers in needed improvements is clearly valuable.

In other universities, non-scheduled or open laboratory hours are made possible by files of videotapes which describe the purposes of experiments and demonstrate the procedures to be followed. Through films or videotapes, it may be possible to simulate some laboratory experiences; however, to date, only instructors in fluid mechanics have made wide use of this method. Many industrial machines and processes which cannot be duplicated on campus might be subjects of well-designed videotape presentations.

The case study method of instruction is gaining favor as an effective way of introducing students to realistic design problems throughout the engineering curriculum. ITV can add realism and emotional stimulation to this method. Good prototypes are cited which involve human factors in systems design and in professional ethics courses. However, much more needs to be done in this area.

The greatest impact of ITV in engineering education to date has been in its off-campus applications. During the past decade, approximately 30 universities have developed regional ITV systems which today provide regular graduate classes originating from campuses to over 44,000 engineers at their job sites. These programs are popular, effective, and continue to proliferate. No federal funds are involved. Rather, these ITV systems are local responses to a professional need and are paid for by industrial and government employers.

Recently, 22 universities, which account for over 85 percent of the off-campus ITV instruction, joined together to form the Association for Media-Based Continuing Education for Engineers (AMCEE). The goal of AMCEE is to increase the national effectiveness of continuing education for engineers. Work is underway to distribute videotaped courses nationally (over 450 courses from 22 universities were cataloged in 1980) and to develop special workshops and seminars on timely topics. The emergence of videopublishing offers the university a unique opportunity to serve the practicing professional.

There are examples of television employed in engineering education at junior colleges, high schools, and in foreign locations. These show considerable promise, but, unfortunately, they are rare.

The use of satellites offers a unique opportunity to develop both nationwide programs and resource sharing with foreign educators. The engineering profession brings a background of tried and tested educational services to the "new" communications technologies. Experiments have already shown that use of satellites could overcome three current types of problems in ITV operations: technical, i.e., the ITV signal can travel only a short distance at a reasonable cost; logistical, i.e., the mail and other delivery services are slow; and financial, i.e., a videotape inventory is expensive. In addition, unique features such as teleconferencing could assist in the co-management of education tasks both between U.S. industries and universities and between foreign universities and U.S. universities. The domestic applications have been studied in detail by AMCEE; satellite delivery of ITV could break even financially two to four years from initiation if capital were available for the ground facilities.

The very recent advent of personal computers and inexpensive videodisc systems, coupled with microprocessors, is stimulating renewed interest in computer-assisted instruction (CAI). University presidents may welcome this consumer "takeover" of computing. During the 1976-77 academic year, $991 million was spent on computers for universities. About three-quarters of this amount came from university funds, and the remainder was primarily supplied by federal agencies. Fewer than 50 engineering colleges recently reported some use of CAI, but virtually all (238) reported use of computers for problem-solving activities.

Very few educators have the experience necessary to make effective use of the new CAI hardware immediately. The first task is, therefore, to enlarge the group of engineering and physical science faculty who study and test the potential of the medium in small working groups at many universities. Like all technology, ET requires key human resources for implementation. The appropriate adoption of ET is seriously hindered by the historical lack of a broad-scale, sustained effort to enlarge the number of talented individuals working with media.

The greatest payoff of the new hardware in engineering education will be attained through interactive computing combined with graphics. These can provide unique learning experiences that will develop skills in synthesizing and analyzing, as well as assist in visualizing, thus developing intuitive skills. Applications of computer-aided design (CAD) and computer-aided manufacturing (CAM) need to be introduced virtually in all of the engineering colleges that today lack the instructional facilities to serve students properly. This is a pressing, massive problem; it needs to be addressed squarely.

The rapid introduction of measuring instruments that incorporate microprocessors and digital memory is widening the gap between industrial practice and university laboratories. The emergence of these powerful new instruments and control devices is outpacing the equipment budgets of universities. Traditional laboratory procedures are being changed fundamentally by the built-in data analysis programs of the instrumentation. Unlike most of the ET discussed in this report in which courseware is the dominant issue, the instrument revolution described above is essentially a hardware problem.

Suggested Actions

Educational technology today offers many attractive investment opportunities. Successful applications of ET in engineering education involve faculty who have both an educator's insight into pedagogical issues and an engineer's skill in organizing and adapting hardware. Perhaps no better proving ground for instructional technology could be devised.

The primary purpose of this report is to provide a critical evaluation of the ET literature with respect to its applications to engineering education. A number of suggestions are made throughout the report and are summarized in Chapter V in the hope that they will serve as stimuli for thoughtful consideration and, perhaps, even action. The authors' principle suggestions, listed in order of priority, are:

- Government agencies should design funding programs which encourage broad-scale, diversified development and testing of ET courseware in various media at the local course level. Although some basic instructional research in artificial intelligence and other, similar areas should be funded, major support should be given to improving local courses and to productivity studies. The purpose of these programs would be to involve many more faculty, nationwide, in meaningful ET activities.
- At least twelve prototype computer graphics centers should be funded in the next two years at selected engineering colleges. These centers would serve as regional models for the organization and operation of interdisciplinary facilities, as clearinghouses for vendors and educators, and as developers of outreach materials for engineering educators nationwide. External funding of these pioneering centers might require one-third to one-quarter local matching funds. A second round of facility grants to ensure the general availability of computer graphic equipment might involve as much as a 50 percent match by colleges and universities.
- Several university videopresses should be endowed at universities having both a strong commitment to continuing education of professionals and the media expertise to set high

standards of quality. These new enterprises would provide a creative outlet for faculty everywhere and encourage the development of modern instructional programs under the guidance of skilled staff.

- An operational plan to test the cost effectiveness of communications satellites should be funded to provide engineers with the following educational services at their job sites: national delivery of graduate credit courses in a coordinated program initially involving 10 AMCEE universities; delivery of continuing education short courses; and teleconferencing between originating sites to provide for direct faculty exchanges, special seminars, and technical meetings. Studies should be undertaken to involve ethnic minority colleges of engineering in activities of their choosing.
- Post-graduate study programs offered by U.S. engineering colleges might be transmitted overseas via satellite. The potential advantages of high-quality educational opportunities available in the homeland of the student may warrant the investment necessary to employ modern communications technology.
- An in-depth study of the equipment problems of colleges of engineering should be undertaken, perhaps by an industrial team sponsored by the National Research Council. Recommendations might include government incentives to industry, as well as emergency programs to overcome what has become a massive problem of hardware acquisition.
- Federal agencies should design a number of new programs to expedite the transition to decentralized computing. These diverse efforts might include sponsorship of the following: consumers' unions to evaluate machines and courseware; visiting lectureships; workshops and summer institutes; and media-based, packaged, short courses for in-service training of teachers.
- Foundations should explore the creation of working consortia or nonprofit organizations to produce high quality films and videotapes in support of case study instruction, especially in engineering design and in professional ethics.
- The use of ET in attracting, motivating, and preparing ethnic minority students and others who are educationally disadvantaged in grades 9 through 12 should be extended. A few university-based centers could supply materials and information to the many programs which are now sponsored by businessmen and educators regionally.
- The National Academy of Engineering (NAE) should sponsor a feasibility study on the creation of several regional computation centers for engineering research.
- The NAE should update its 1974 study on issues and public policies in ET in the light of current trends and forecasts in hardware delivery systems.

I.
EDUCATIONAL TECHNOLOGY

The promise of technology in the educational process at all levels has never been greater than it is today. The reason is clear: the microelectronics revolution of the past decade, together with digital and laser system development, is just starting to bear fruit in useful instructional hardware. The cost of such hardware continues to decrease and may soon be an insignificant impediment. Now, the challenge of devising appropriate ways to employ hardware in education is brought into sharper focus.

Educational technology (ET) encompasses two aspects: the organization of knowledge for learners; and the use of materials and machines to aid in the learning process. Educational technologists are those who seek to apply scientific and other organized knowledge to the practical tasks of education. These creative practitioners endeavor to understand learning theory and to apply it. They often are viewed by their peers as reformers, even revolutionists. However, perhaps most fairly, many ET activists are proselytizing optimists! Their optimism now seems warranted since more ET alternatives are rapidly becoming affordable.

For a variety of reasons, however, the practice of ET falls short of the promise envisioned by some people. Cost is often cited today as a major impediment to computer-based instruction. Yet, economically attractive alternatives such as some forms of instructional television (ITV) have not gained universal acceptance. The effectiveness of ET varies from situation to situation, but ET is often on par with traditional methods. Lack of wide acceptance of ET is sometimes traced to conservative institutions of higher education in which, it is argued, neither faculty nor administrators have the appropriate experience and knowledge needed to introduce ET effectively. Continuing this line of thought, some ET enthusiasts state that traditional schools are obsolete and that ET can, in principle, provide educational services to widely dispersed learners in a time-independent manner. More thoughtful educators argue that the premise that suitable ET is readily available today is incorrect. The delivery devices may be purchased perhaps, but instructional materials are rarely marketed. Furthermore, the development and

6

introduction of ET should be matched carefully to learner needs. ET extremists are viewed as classical examples of technologists in search of problems.

The literature review which follows focuses on ET in practice, starting with a brief historical overview. The body of the material is organized by specific delivery technologies, i.e., video, computer/video combinations, and communications satellites. Under each technology, illustrative examples of applications in various settings are presented. Where available, evaluative and economic data are cited with each example. Because this report covers a wide range of materials, readers seeking information on a specific topic should first scan the Table of Contents.

The core of the ET organizational problem is fundamental: all learning is individual, even in group instructional settings; individuals vary greatly in characteristics; and the behavior of each person may vary over time and be subject to complex environmental influences. David Hawkridge, Director of the Institute of Educational Technology of the Open University of the United Kingdom, states the problem candidly:

> One of the questions I am frequently asked by visitors to the Open University is, "How do you choose which media to use for different parts of your multi-media courses?"
>
> I feel that I am expected, in answer, to point to a beautifully constructed algorithm and explain how a carefully balanced analysis of pedagogical factors leads to the best choice. In fact, I have to admit that no such algorithm or analysis exists, and that the University's selections of media are controlled by logistical, financial, and internal political factors rather than by soundly based and clearly specified psychological and pedagogical considerations.
>
> I don't like admitting this: it seems as though it is not to the credit of the University, a leader in the multi-media field. But, I don't feel too defensive about it. The fact is that instructional researchers and designers have not provided even the foundations for constructing strong practical procedures for selecting media appropriate to given learning tasks. If there has been British work in this area, I have been unable to discover it. . . . In the United States, over 2,000 media studies have not yielded the answers we need. (Hawkridge, n.d.)

Infancy of ET: 1950 to 1965

Hawkridge (1976) captures the spirit of ET in practice. He reviews the conceptual framework from the point of view of an educational

psychologist, and, in a lively fashion, puts today's efforts into
historical perspective. He notes that Skinner's (1954) principles for
teaching machines, including programmed texts/machines, were the
hallmark of ET in its infancy:

- Reinforce the student's responses frequently and immediately;
- Provide for the student to be in control of the learning rate;
- Make sure the student follows a coherent, controlled sequence; and
- Require participation through responding.

Programmed instruction has a small but dedicated following among
engineering educators. One technique, which generally follows these
principles, has gained wide acceptance in engineering education. This
pedagogy, personalized system of instruction (PSI), is discussed in
detail later, but the close relationship between PSI and early
educational research is worthy of note. In citing Hartley's (1974)
systematic review of research on programmed learning, Hawkridge notes:
"No method of instruction has ever come into use surrounded by so much
research activity."

From 1949 to 1953, a group of college professors interested in
educational psychology met annually to develop a taxonomy of behavioral
objectives in the cognitive domain. The resulting book, Bloom (1956),
has had a significant and continuing influence on curriculum
development at all levels. Reference is made to this taxonomy in the
later discussion of computer-based instruction for engineers.

During this early period, researchers in psychometrics refined
testing methods along two lines, norm-referenced and criterion-
referenced testing. Hawkridge (1976) observes that "a full
understanding of the differences between the two types of tests has
continued to elude many [ET] practitioners." Norm-referenced tests are
intended to show where a student stands in relation to a peer group,
and, in many cases, the statistical work behind the test development
assumes a normal distribution of ability among students.
Criterion-referenced testing, on the other hand, assumes that a given
task can be achieved at a given criterion level by all who have been
appropriately taught. The latter form is almost exclusively used by
engineering educators. There is one notable exception, the nationally
administered Engineer in Training (EIT) examination. The EIT is the
first step toward registration of professional engineers and is
intended, among other things, to protect public safety and welfare. In
this light, one might reasonably expect a criterion-referenced test,
but, in fact, the current program employs an norm-referenced test. It
is safe to say that psychometric research has had little influence on
engineering educators.

Adolescence of ET: 1965 to Date

By the mid-1960's, interest shifted from programmed learning to
other formats. Hawkridge (1976) found that fewer and fewer programs
were written strictly according to Skinner's original prescription.

The pure linear program, consisting of many short frames with a high degree of repetition, was no longer favored. Crowderian branching was inserted into linear sequences more often as pointed out by Lumsdale and Glaser (1960). Hawkridge (1976) notes that "Educators and psychologists were saying that the only machines which stood a chance of succeeding commercially were those which incorporated more than the written word, through using records, tape, or film." The literature of the day talked of multi-media systems design, as well as behavioral objectives.

Computer-assisted instruction (CAI) was slowly gaining supporters. During the mid-1960's, for example, most engineering colleges had only central, batch operated computers available, and, in many locations, the selection of equipment and its operation was in the hands of administrative data processors. In a benchmark publication (Buchnell and Allen, 1967), the role of computers in higher education was assessed and directions for the future were outlined:

> Some assume (correctly) that the production of time-sharing programs can be quite expensive, and on the other hand, some assume (incorrectly) that time-sharing systems are available as off-the-shelf items. Someday they may be, and a few, such as those of General Electric, almost are. Indeed, most major computer systems eventually will be delivered with at least the framework for a time-shared system, but we should not be overly optimistic about the rapidity with which these can be put into operation. (Buchnell and Allen, 1967)

Nonetheless, work to individualize instruction (CAI) was well underway. A review of the systems and projects (ibid., Chapter 8, Karl L. Zinn) discusses the functions of CAI systems and catalogs 26 major projects then in progress.

If computers in education attracted technical specialists and others who were often favorably disposed to the programmed learning approach, television did not. Films are the natural antecedent of instructional television (ITV), and many of the early practitioners came to ITV from film making. Not surprisingly, artistic values play a large role in the ITV research literature; quality is often judged in the context of the audiovisual impact of the medium. Taking this a step farther, a well-respected producer of ITV programs argues that the printed material should take care of the cognitive aspects of learning and the ITV program should take care of the emotional aspects of the matter (R. Lundgren, Chapter I, in W. Schramm, 1972). Conversely, the "talking head" is synonymous with bad television, because, the argument goes, ITV should have the same stimulating impact that the learner has come to expect from commercial TV. While these attitudes are maintained to this day by an articulate group, ITV in engineering education takes many forms, ranging from inexpensive, candid classroom presentations to expensive British Broadcasting Company (BBC) documentaries. Engineering educators seem not to be influenced by the experimental research on ITV, perhaps because many of the so-called

experiments simply are gross comparisons of factual recall by students
receiving ITV instruction with control groups of students receiving
conventional classroom instruction. Often, this comparison reveals no
significant differences even though the attitudes of the students may
have been affected significantly.

"In contrast to the hundreds of experimental comparisons of ITV
with conventional classroom teaching reported in the literature, there
are, at most, a few score of studies specifically on the content and
strategies of ITV." (Schramm, 1972) By enriching this data base with
earlier studies of films, Schramm concludes "that the research on
content variables comes down very strongly on two points which offer
useful guidelines to anyone concerned with programming instructional
television or film. One of these is simplicity of presentation; the
other, active participation by student in the learning experience."
(ibid.) Appendix A reproduces more conclusions from Schramm's study
which should be of interest to engineering educators. These
conclusions provide a thoughtful antidote for the film maker's folklore.

The introduction of instructional technology often occurs without
an explicit statement of goals. More often than not, the rationale for
a given approach in a university is determined either by a single
professor or by a small faculty group, which may have multiple,
unarticulated goals. At the local administrative level, when specific
resources are available, the task is to select the policies, people,
facilities, and equipment that will give the students the best and
biggest education per buck. Educational technologists argue that the
current ad hoc practices could be improved by a systems approach, which
also often implies a team of specialists working in a closely
coordinated fashion (e.g., Pask and Lewis, 1972; or, for research
background, Merrill, 1971). Conceptually, the systems approach should
be attractive to engineering educators. However, just as a creative
engineering designer may proceed through the steps in a systems
approach while directing a design project, though perhaps not
sequentially, documentation often is sparse, particularly in smaller
organizations. A systems specialist may not be available, yet the
project is completed. Unfortunately, the engineering educator
frequently fails in this respect also. Yet, there is no serious debate
about the need for a conceptual framework or the desirability of
documentation. The few exceptions in which documentation of a systems
approach exists are worth noting; these are drawn from widely differing
approaches to engineering education (Rosenstein, 1968; Wales and
Stager, 1972; Keller and Koen, 1976).

Economics of ET

The systems approach places appropriate emphasis on an explicit
statement of instructional objectives and measurement of outcomes to
determine whether these objectives have been met. In this context,
policy-makers can view the introduction of technology in economic terms.

Unfortunately, when technology is externally imposed, instructors
often fear "automation" of the educational process and interpret this

in the coldest possible terms, i.e., operational cost savings by
replacing teachers with machines which require only a capital
investment (Starke, 1972). There are, of course, many other
economically attractive ways to employ technology, but, since these are
often poorly understood by administrators and faculty alike, the
economic concepts involved remain largely abstractions.

Productivity is a concept related to the amount of output one gets
from inputs to a production process (Melmed, 1973 and Haggerty, 1974).
Few educators are satisfied with student-credit-hours as the sole
output measure for higher education, and rightfully so, because
credit-hour production totally lacks a measure of quality. While we
appear "stuck" with this proxy in national or macro-economic studies,
at the course or curriculum level, better productivity measures are
possible. Indeed, it is hard to deny that cost allocations on the
input side have reached some degree of sophistication in higher
education.

An excellent example of productivity studies which demonstrate the
power of the concept and the variety of relationships which can be
described in tangible terms is the work of Willey (1975) on
instructional computing. Appendix B reproduces these case studies.
Productivity is a promising framework for judging the effectiveness of
instructional technology. It places a burden on academe to document
activity, but it offers an accountability measure understood by
policy-makers, or at least their staffs. Educators surely should be
interested in the examples that demonstrate that, although computing
increased rather than decreased the current costs of instruction,
outputs could be identified which justified the additional inputs.

While it is tempting, the argument that these ideas can be readily
extended to show that the input combinations chosen for a task are the
minimum cost choice, or that we know how to design the most _efficient_
educational program is premature (Jamison, _et al._, 1974). The dilemma
posed by no significant difference in outcome between traditional
classroom instruction and various forms of instructional technology is
that any search for the most efficient mix of instructional methods
surely will be in the direction of the least expensive formats. Yet,
few of us would want to endure a regular diet of large lecture courses,
perhaps interspersed with inexpensive ITV or PSI. Schramm (1977)
examines the issues associated with the selection and blending of
instructional technologies in depth, and, while he offers no easy
answers, he does offer sound advice to decision-makers at all levels.

Instructional Goals for ET

In the conviction that technology can make education more
productive, individual, and powerful, make learning more
immediate, give instruction more scientific base, and make
access to education more equal, the Commission concludes
that the nation should increase its investment in
instructional technology, thereby upgrading the quality of
education, and, ultimately, the quality of individuals'
lives and of society generally.

Our study has shown that one-shot injections of a single technological medium are ineffective. At best they offer only optional "enrichment." Technology, we believe, can carry out its full potential for education only insofar as educators embrace instructional technology as a system and integrate a range of human and nonhuman resources into the total educational process. (Tickton, 1970)

A short list of the most common instructional goals for ET in engineering education follows:

- To reduce or contain costs (replace teachers and/or administrators);
- To enrich, improve, and individualize instruction; and
- To serve the unserved or enlarge coverage.

These are not mutually exclusive, of course, and the list might be expanded. The list does indicate, however, the most important objectives for modern technological methods in engineering education.

The balance of this brief report will focus primarily on television. In part, the backgrounds of the authors dictate this, but the outcome should not be distorted. The role of computers and computing in education is much better documented in the literature, no doubt because the investment required is massive in comparison to that for television. Furthermore, the videodisc, which stimulates much of the current interest in ET, is exciting because it may offer a hybrid of these media at an affordable cost.

II.

VIDEO-BASED INSTRUCTION

In 1966, an equipment breakthrough occurred in video recorders. Ampex introduced a one-inch videotape recorder/player for about $3,000. The unit delivered good quality displays if properly maintained, though the early machines were only about 80 to 90 percent reliable. Redundance overcame this problem because the price was right. Indeed, the only good quality black-and-white video recorders available prior to this model were priced at $50,000 to $100,000. Several Japanese manufacturers introduced one-half-inch tape recorders in 1967, and, after a brief period, settled on a standard format (EIAJ). These compatible machines sold for about $800, and, like the earlier one-inch tape machines, they required careful maintenance. Sony Corporation introduced a three-quarter-inch videocassette in 1970, inducing other manufacturers to promote compatible units, indeed almost identical machines. Tape handling, head wear, and other maintenance problems were greatly reduced in these units which now sell for $1,000 to $1,500. The fidelity of the recordings and the flexibility provided to the user are both excellent. The most recent recorder to be marketed is targeted for consumer/home use. The one-half-inch cassette units come in two formats, Beta and VHS (the Philips unit is still another); these were first widely offered in 1977 by at least eight manufacturers within a price range of $800 to $1,200. Unfortunately, the two formats are not compatible, and, since various tape speeds are employed as well, this product offers potential problems to the user unless local standardization is enforced.

A block diagram of the major components of an instructional television system (ITV) is shown in Figure 1. The reproducer/playback units are now a part of many systems because of the improved cost/performance cited above. As Figure 1 indicates, a variety of over-the-air systems is employed today by engineering educators. Standard public broadcast facilities for educational television are available on a limited basis in several state-wide systems. Instructional television fixed service (ITFS) is specifically designated by the Federal Communications Commission (FCC) for ITV applications. Operating at a frequency of 2.5 gigahertz, ITFS has

13

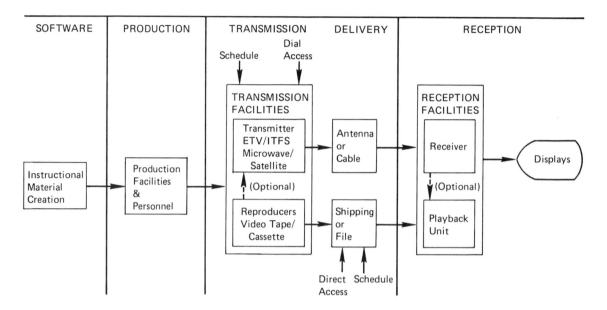

SOURCE: Hayman and Levin, 1973.

FIGURE 1 Instructional television systems.

4 megahertz bandwidth with up to 40 broadcast channels set aside. In 1980, however, the FCC proposes to lower this allocation. These systems are quite reliable and operate over a 30- to 40-mile radius; two to four channel capacity systems start at $500,000. Point-to-point microwave systems operating at 12 gigahertz are employed by a few systems with retransmission installations every 15 to 20 miles along a highly directional beam. At least one university system employs cable television delivery (CATV) off campus, and CATV is a common on-campus technology (Ward, 1974). There is no routine use of satellite transmission at this time in engineering education, though some experiments and planning efforts have been carried out, as is discussed later.

> As long as it is used in the broadcast mode, television is limited to real time reception. When recording techniques were developed and extended to the storage and playback of color images, however, the requirement for simultaneous sending and receiving gave way to the possibility of allowing each function to be performed independently. The addition of time independence to distance viewing has alleviated a major hurdle to the use of television by educators. (Miller and Baldwin, 1975)

The choice of a delivery system without talkback in a given region around a university for minimum cost follows these general guidelines: widely scattered, small class sections tend to favor videotape; small classes concentrated in a geographic radius of 30 to 40 miles tend to favor ITFS, if channel capacity is available; and large installations, over 50 miles distant, tend to favor either point-to-point microwave or videotape depending on frequency of use (Loomis and Brandt, 1973). Yet, there are numerous exceptions in practice, and, as the specific examples cited below illustrate, there are good reasons for these exceptions.

Applications to Engineering Education On Campus

Instructional television on campus may substitute for a live lecturer or provide review and remedial study opportunities. Videotape provides the schedule flexibility needed to support self-paced instruction in the classroom, as well as in laboratory orientation. ITV has several applications in design courses. Finally, students report improved skills in oral presentations and job interviewing techniques when given the opportunity to view videotape replays.

Lectures/Presentations

The use of television on campus often takes the form of lectures and presentations. Some examples will illustrate the wide diversity of on-campus applications.

Regular Classes: Pennsylvania State University pioneered the use of ITV on campus starting in the mid-1950's with CATV to classrooms and dormitories. C. R. Carpenter (1958) reported on these early efforts. Here and elsewhere in the early trials, ITV often was used to present entire lectures in a traditional course. No significant differences in learning were reported initially in these studies. However, the students did gain great flexibility in selecting the time and place for viewing the lectures. Lecture preparation and videotaping took place in a university TV studio; however, production conditions were usually spartan.

In 1971, the Rochester Institute of Technology (RIT) produced a sophomore course in engineering mechanics (Statics) in its TV studios. The 45-minute lectures, the coordinated textbook, and the student workbooks were developed by two RIT faculty in a team teaching approach. The four-credit course employed three ITV lectures a week viewed without proctors from a campus CATV system in small classrooms or dormitories on a very flexible schedule. Cassettes also were filed in the library for individual viewing. The two faculty members met with small groups of students in recitation/problem sessions once a week for two hours as a live supplement to the taped lectures. The performance of the students on examinations was unchanged compared to the previous history of conventional instruction in this course. The department personnel believed the course design and coordinated materials to be superior to those employed prior to 1971. Because the two faculty members were freed from lecturing, they were able to teach more students and to answer questions on a more individual basis than had been the case in the conventional program. Over the four-year experimental period, the costs of initial production plus recitations was lower than the traditional alternative. Nevertheless, the course reverted to a traditional classroom format in 1976 because many sophomores objected to the use of ITV. More than half did not attend the lectures during the last year of the program; rather, they relied on the printed materials and recitation periods (Kenyon, 1978).

At Colorado State University (CSU), a similar test of ITV for the sophomore core course in electrical engineering drew strong criticism from the students in 1969. However, in this case "the tapes were, at best, plain. There was little use of visuals, there was no rehearsal, there was no director, and there was little effort given to making tapes of professional broadcast quality." (Neidt, 1970) Student performance was assessed, of course, but no control group was maintained for comparison. The course also employed a new, more mathematical approach so that no meaningful comparisons with the performance of students during previous years could be made. In 1970, the course reverted to traditional instruction, using another textbook.

The attitude of undergraduates toward ITV lectures is frequently unenthusiastic despite the fact that learning is not impaired and, in some cases, is enhanced. One of the most sustained efforts on record is the use of ITV for a first year course in accounting at CSU. The objectives stated for this course in 1964 were to:

- Combat the shortage of qualified instructors;
- Bring the instruction of seasoned teachers to large numbers of students through the use of television;
- Standardize the content of elementary accounting courses;
- Provide uniform instruction, testing, and grading;
- Keep classes relatively small;
- Persuade graduate students to become teachers;
- Permit staff members to experiment with new ideas and communication methods; and
- Maintain or improve instructional quality at reduced cost. (McCosh, 1970)

After some experimentation, the course has been refined. Approximately 40 percent of the course now comprises taped lectures that last from 20 to 30 minutes each. The lectures are produced in a studio, and selected portions are redone annually to ensure that the material is up to date. The visual content, e.g., the use of highlights and color for emphasis, is excellent in the current series. Graduate teaching assistants proctor the CATV-delivered lectures in classes of approximately 30 students each; the assistant serves as a tutor for the remainder of each 50-minute period. A printed study guide, which incorporates the lecture visuals, supplements the textbook. For 14 years, this method has been employed for all students in beginning accounting. CSU students who receive this training score well on the norm-referenced Achievement Test, Level I, of the American Institute of Certified Public Accountants.

Over 100 universities, including some of the best, participate in this national examination; the mean grade of CSU students is consistently in the top 25th percentile. Yet, a common student complaint is that "the presentations are somewhat dry and boring."

A survey of 135 departments of accounting in 1973 showed that: 95 had never tried ITV; 15 had tried it but dropped it; and 10 planned to use it but had no previous experience. Only 15 were using ITV, had never abandoned its use, and were planning to continue using it. Some of the impediments cited by the respondents were:

- Students complained that ITV was too impersonal;
- Faculty argued that ITV, as compared to traditional methods, often did not appear to improve learning (the CSU example is contrary to the findings reported in the general literature where no significant difference in outcome is often found);
- Administrators argued lack of facilities and equipment; and
- Faculty incentives were often lacking, e.g., no publication credit for ITV production, and no release time to prepare the ITV lectures. (McCosh, 1978)

This list of impediments illustrates an important feature of ITV in universities today. <u>Well documented courses covering standard material are not generally exchanged among universities</u>. The implicit assumption is that each school will develop its own courses, though most producers presumably could arrange for the lease or sale of materials if requested. Lauer (1978) publishes <u>THE</u> <u>Catalog</u> which lists 550 ITV courses in an effort to stimulate wider use of available materials.

Students react far more favorably when they elect to take an ITV course. Sanford B. Thayer developed 10 half-hour lectures on engineering economy which were studio-produced in color at CSU. A 260-page study guide for the course was prepared to complement a nationally popular text book; it included all of the visuals from the lecture, as well as problem sets with solutions. In 1975, 18 of 72 seniors enrolled on campus chose to take the two-semester course by individual study using the ITV materials. On the three examinations given during the semester, the regular class, which was devoting 30 class hours to the course, scored slightly higher than the ITV students. However, the magnitude of the difference reached the 0.05 level of significance on the second test only. "It would appear the video class learned nearly as much as the regular class. The video class members spent less time on the course than the regular class and also were able to work on it at their convenience. Considering these trade-offs, the videopublished version compares quite favorably with the regular class." (Sjogren, <u>et</u> <u>al</u>., 1976)

From the economic point of view, the ITV picture is bright. With the variety of available approaches to course production and delivery, it is rather easy to present ITV lectures on campus for $1.00 to $3.00 per student-contact-hour (Hayman and Levin, 1973). For the introductory accounting course cited above, the lectures cost about $1.17 per student-contact-hour.

Consider an extreme, hypothetical case. A department could purchase the Thayer engineering economy tapes for $2,485. A videoplayer, color monitor, and cart may cost $1,700. If the department serves only 200 students during the life of this equipment, this coursework (10 half-hour classes) will cost $4.00 per student-contact-hour. (As is customary in higher education, the interest cost of having money invested in capital equipment is neglected in this calculation. If added, the capital equipment base price would increase by approximately 15 percent. Neglecting interest, of course, favors ET over traditional methods.) Very few engineering colleges can teach senior level courses in the traditional way for less than this amount. When more realistic usage of the playback equipment is assumed, the cost of the transmission, delivery, and reception portion of the ITV system quickly becomes negligible. Conservatively, the portable unit described above could cost less than $0.10 per student-contact-hour. In other words, as a first approximation, the cost of ITV on campus can be estimated solely on the amortization of the courseware or cassette. This principle is not new; it has been applied to educational films for years.

An ITV lecture replayed in a classroom may not be the most attractive application of this technology, except from the point of view of reducing costs. ITV has some unique features that permit a variety of interesting applications as the remainder of the examples illustrates.

Lecture Review: The transition from high school to university study is difficult for many students. The failure rate for ethnic minority freshmen in some engineering colleges is alarmingly high. The Massachusetts Institute of Technology (MIT) has employed tutored videotaped instruction (TVI) to address this problem with excellent results. The objectives of the MIT program are: 1) to offer academic support to a selected group of first year minority students in Physics 8.02; 2) to measure the effectiveness of tutored videotape instruction (TVI) as a secondary pedagogical aid; and 3) to determine the transferability to subjects similar to Physics 8.02. Some freshmen were invited to attend both regular lectures and TVI sessions, which lasted two hours each and were held on the same day as the formal lecture. Professor Wesley L. Harris, Sr., reports:

> The concept of instruction of students in the presence of a tutor from videotapes of formal lectures is revolutionary at the very least. From the observation of students immersed in this form of instruction, I feel that this format has great potential. It may actually prove more effective than the traditional lecture/recitation format if given the proper opportunity. From the comments I have heard the students make, the ability to stop a lecture when there is a question in one's mind is far superior to the formal lecture....the personal contact between students and tutor is much more effective than receiving instruction from an impersonal lecturer. In other words, learning from someone you know is much easier than learning from a stranger. (Salloway, 1978)

None of the ten students who participated in TVI received a failing grade, but 25 percent of the minority students who did not participate did receive failing grades.

Videotapes of classroom lectures are used by individual students in a wide variety of settings. The objective often is to provide either a review or remedial opportunities. Direct access to the tapes and playback units may be provided in individual study carrels in the library or in special study areas. Case Western Reserve University, CSU and MIT employ CATV to dormitories to deliver videotaped lectures which supplement lectures in certain core courses. CSU found that only about 25 percent of its freshmen reported using the system, though it is wired into every room. Live tutors at the dormitory in the evening, on the other hand, drew an 80 percent response. Freshmen cited lack of time as a major deterrent. Faculty did not encourage use of the CATV by integrating the taped lectures into the course requirements, nor did they actively discourage its use (Britton and Schweizer, 1974). MIT has some live recitation periods in its campus system with professors answering telephone questions.

Worcester Polytechnic Institute encourages individual study by using ITV in a number of ways. Although a relatively small school, Worcester Polytechnic has 75 to 100 students who use 25 carrels daily to receive supplemental instruction. The videotapes are usually direct and are considered to be almost a visual memoranda by the faculty to students who need additional explanations, data for a problem assignment, or instruction on laboratory procedures (Scott, et al., 1974).

Special ITV classrooms decribed later under off-campus programs operate on about 30 campuses today. Several schools report that campus students are increasingly requesting an opportunity to view tapes made of senior and graduate level lectures. The reasons most often given for the replay requests are to make up missed lectures and to review material.

Summer Session Classes: Summer session presents an annual problem in some engineering colleges due to unpredictable or small enrollments. CSU has resorted to making videotapes in special video-equipped classrooms of several freshmen and sophomore core courses while these are being taught during the regular academic year. The courses are announced in the summer bulletin as programs guaranteed to be offered regardless of enrollment. If enrollments exceed a stated minimum, usually 15 to 20, then the instructor may teach the class in the traditional manner if the class prefers (always) and receive full salary coverage. When the enrollment fails to reach the minimum, the faculty member meets with the class weekly for a two-hour recitation period for half salary and relies on the tapes which he made earlier in the year for the lecture sessions. Students accept this procedure as a good alternative to cancelling courses due to low enrollments. By agreement with the faculty, the tapes are erased at the end of each summer period. The practice of erasing tapes made in the candid classroom mode is universal. On the one hand, faculty do not want the lectures stored for long periods; on the other hand, a very massive tape inventory otherwise would be required.

<u>Classroom Demonstrations</u>: Distance seeing (television) is a unique characteristic that is well suited to instruction in engineering graphics. At Iowa State University, the instructor lectures and demonstrates from a drafting table in direct view of the students. His drafting table has an overhead television camera with controls alongside the table. Each pair of students at a drafting table views an 11-inch TV monitor. In this way, the instructor can face the students while they have a direct, over-the-shoulder view of his illustrations and technique. This drafting room table system has been modified to include a video-cassette player input, making possible the use of modular, studio produced, color instruction by videotape. With this system, instructor time can be devoted to tutorial interactions rather than to presenting lectures (Eide, 1971; 1974). Biology and medical educators have used the unique viewing capability of ITV in a similar manner with great success.

Self-Paced Instruction

Pedagogy which requires self-pacing of study can be mediated using ITV. Perhaps the most popular version is the personalized system of instruction (PSI). The features are:

- The go-at-your-own-pace feature, which permits a student to move through the course at a speed commensurate with his/her ability and other demands upon his/her time;
- The unit-perfection requirement for advance, which lets the student go ahead to new material only after demonstrating mastery of that which preceded;
- The uses of lectures and demonstrations as vehicles of motivation, rather than sources of critical information;
- The related stress upon the written word in teacher-student communication; and, finally,
- The use of proctors, which permits repeated testing, immediate scoring, almost unavoidable tutoring, and a marked enhancement of the personal-social aspect of the educational process. (Stice, ed., 1971)

Figure 2 outlines PSI; each unit forms a set of activities along the lines shown. Traditionally, the instructional media is print. A typical unit contains a reading assignment, study questions, collateral references, study problems, and any necessary introductory and explanatory material.

<u>Role of ITV</u>: Opportunities exist for non-print media, as well (Keller and Koen, 1976). For example, the pre-calculus mathematics course at CSU employs ITV. The decision to use ITV was based on the observation that many students learn mathematical operations by watching a teacher do problems.

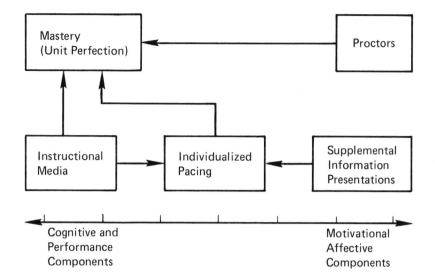

SOURCE: Keller and Koen, 1976.

FIGURE 2 Keller's personalized system of
instruction (PSI).

An instructional system developed specifically for the
pre-calculus program at CSU enrolls more than 5,000
students each fall semester. This system incorporates the
mastery-learning, self-paced features of PSI, but avoids
the high cost, labor intensity of PSI. Individual
examinations, under this system, are scored by a computer
rather than by a tutor. Immediate feedback is still
provided to the student, however, by printing detailed
solutions to the exams in advance and giving them to each
student as he/she leaves the testing room.

PSI-like study guides (known locally as "Survival
Manuals") are sold through the bookstore. Individual
tutoring is available on a walk-in basis throughout the
day in the Mathematics Learning Center.

In this system, the content of the usual college
pre-calculus has been divided into eight one-credit
courses. This arrangement, coupled with a testing program
for all entering students, makes it possible to
accommodate students entering with different levels of
preparation as well as to tailor individual programs for
students pursuing non-engineering, as well as engineering
majors who are making up deficiencies.

A variety of learning styles as well as learning rates are
also provided for by making available several learning
resources which students can use in any combination of

their choice. The resources available include "live" lectures, printed materials, individual tutoring, and now, for the first time, video tapes. The effect of introducing these video tapes remains to be seen, but we are expecting it to reduce the demand for expensive "live" lectures while providing more flexibility of schedule for students learning a self-paced mode. (Brumley, 1978)

The economics of PSI are similar to university ITV in that the cost of courseware preparation dominates. Delivery costs to the university can be relatively small. However, a course which requires the purchase of two or three textbooks is not inexpensive for the college student today.

Books as ET: Books are by far the most widely adopted form of educational technology. Traditional instruction and PSI rely heavily on printed material for instruction, and the university has been the classical seat of creation of textbooks. For many years, books have been a consumer product. Calculations of the relative cost of media-based instruction often use as a benchmark cost estimates for traditional instruction which include the cost of the required books. Books are no longer negligible items. In fact, today, the books needed to support 450 contact hours of traditional engineering instruction often cost $150 to $200 per academic year. Of course, the student may lower this by reselling books and/or by purchasing used books. The important point, however, is that apparently all the normal economic advantages of scale have been exhausted in this area. Book costs are showing a steady increase over time as indicated by the data in Figure 3 which were taken from Publishers Weekly and plotted by Hayman and Levin (1973). In considering the economics of all types of ET, the cost of books is a crucial factor.

In Appendix C, the comments of C. G. Bowen (1974) are given. He provides an enjoyable discussion of books as the first educational technology.

Laboratory Courses

Media can be used in laboratory courses in a variety of ways. Students' performance on report writing and presentations can be improved through audio and video recordings. Basic instruction in the use of laboratory equipment can be standardized and streamlined. In addition, the unique capabilities of certain ET's enable close viewing of microscopic experiments as well as simulations of experiments, machinery, and processes that cannot be duplicated on today's campuses.

Report Writing and Presentations: Written reports and oral presentations by students are important parts of many engineering laboratory courses. A number of educators have successfully employed media to improve performance. J. P. Holman (1977) and his colleagues at Southern Methodist University require students to submit a blank audio cassette with each laboratory report. The instructor uses the

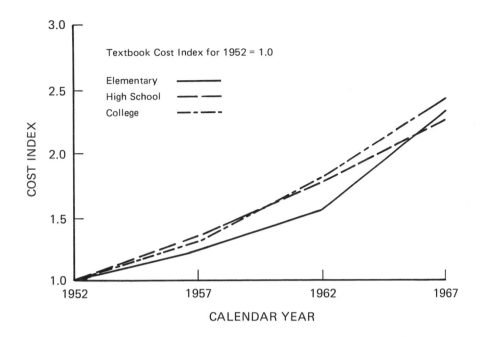

SOURCE: Hayman and Levin, 1973.

FIGURE 3   Textbook cost trend.

audio cassette to record comments which are keyed on the student's written report by red penciled numbers and underlined passages. Voice tone adds a fresh dimension to the tutoring. Of even more importance, the relative speed of speaking versus writing makes the task less time consuming and more complete. This is a very effective technique, since virtually all students either own or have easy access to a cassette player.

Several colleges employ video equipped classrooms or portapaks (one-half-inch EIAJ recorders with inexpensive cameras) to record student presentations (Barile, et al., 1977). Some call this microteaching (Perlberg and O'Bryant, 1970). Regardless of the nomenclature, the opportunity to view one's own presentation by replay and to be coached by peers and teachers on needed improvements is valuable. Taken a step further, some students, given the opportunity, become interested in television as an art form and experiment with a wide variety of independent productions through clubs (Salloway, 1978). Just as students who produce the college magazine usually become better writers, students who experiment with readily available and inexpensive TV equipment usually become proficient in the medium. At CSU, the atmospheric science students did the local weather and ski reports on the dormitory CATV. These popular programs included illustrated (graphics and films) mini-lectures on the physical phenomena associated with the weather changes that were predicted to occur.

Equipment Instruction:

> Before starting a laboratory experiment in a first year
> chemistry course at the University of Illinois, Chicago
> Circle, the entire class will view a color video-cassette
> that explains the purpose of the experiment and the
> procedure to be followed, and presents appropriate
> comments or warnings. These tapes, used for each
> experiment, are considered an essential part of the
> laboratory instruction. (Miller and Baldwin, 1975)

The example cited above is representative. Today, many
universities are using ITV in many ways to supplement laboratory
instruction by providing essential information on the use of
laboratory instruments. Unfortunately, these efforts are rarely
documented or shared.

Close Viewing: The unique ability of ITV for close viewing is
well demonstrated by another laboratory example. Students at Iowa
State University learn the electron microscopy of inorganic materials
with the aid of a closed circuit television system. The TV camera is
mounted where the light binoculars customarily are located, and it is
aimed at the fluorescent screen. Demonstrations of the microscope
operation are performed for groups of students, rather than for one or
two as usually is required. Thus, the instructor is able to maintain
contact with each student. Rosauer (1970) gives more details about
demonstrations that are particularly effective.

> In another laboratory application, a video camera is used
> to obtain data from one or more instruments during the
> progress of an experiment. With several monitors, if
> necessary, a large class of students can easily see the
> instruments, take readings at critical points, and use
> the data so obtained to calculate results from the
> experiment.

> This technique is used at the University of Colorado to
> allow Civil Engineering students to observe the dials on
> the large machines that test the strength of materials.
> The dials are not conveniently located and, normally,
> would not be visible to more than two or three students
> at a time. (Miller and Baldwin, 1975)

Simulations: Simulations of laboratory experiments also are
possible. One of the most complete and popular set of materials was
produced by the National Committee for Fluid Mechanics Films. Largely
done in black and white during the 1960's, these films form a rather
complete set of illustrated experiments on the fundamental phenomena of
fluid motion. A paperback set of notes helps the students and faculty
recall and interpret the sound films (Shapiro, et al., 1972). Numerous

film loops on single concepts have been edited from the longer films; all materials are distributed by the Encyclopedia Britannica Educational Corporation. To date, this series surely must be the most widely used set of engineering educational films.

The methodology used to produce the series still serves as a model for ITV curricula development today. It involved broadly selected advisory committees, a principal author, and a trained film crew with experienced directors and editors. The work was carried out through the Educational Development Center, Newton, Massachusetts, with funds from the National Science Foundation and, to a lesser extent, the Office of Naval Research. To encourage professional recognition, The Journal of Fluid Mechanics regularly reviews new contributions to this film library.

Many industrial machines and processes cannot be duplicated on campus. Nonetheless, educators may wish to expose students to certain aspects of current practice. Field trips to neighboring firms may help, but the local selection usually is narrowly limited. Films produced by educators through an organization patterned after the one described above could greatly enlarge such instructional opportunities. The films could involve not only industrial operations but also national government laboratories. Of course, it is essential that clearly stated instructional objectives be identified and that the TV or film production be directed by professionals.

Design: Project Courses

The senior design course is viewed by many educators as the capstone of the undergraduate experience. At least three approaches are employed: project courses (authentic involvement); case studies; and guided design. Koen (1976) discusses each method briefly and gives primary citations in the literature. ITV does not yet play a central role in any of these instructional techniques, but examples can be cited to show its potential.

Project courses are the most common design experience of students. Students learn the art of design by designing. A good insight into the various practices employed across the country is provided by the Proceedings of the Conference on Engineering Design Education entitled "Authentic Involvement in Interdisciplinary Design." (Bulkeley, ed., 1965)

Projects play a central role in the innovative undergraduate program at Worcester Polytechnic Institute. A self-paced, individualized approach is taken in the project activity with the extensive support of do-it-yourself videotapes. For example, the Projects Instrumentation and Measurements Experimental Learning Laboratory consists of a series of mediated modules specifically designed to support students in project activity. The lab is open to students of all disciplines who come to obtain information, and, ultimately, select the method and instruments consistent with their project goal (Scott, 1978).

In some projects which have a high visual content, ITV can become an integral part of the student work. For example, faculty and students of the Department of Urban Studies and Planning at MIT prepared a 16-minute videotape documentary on "Copley Square," a planned development of shopping facilities, convention hotel, and parking (Salloway, 1978). The documentary examined a controversy surrounding a demand issued by community groups that the developer, a Chicago firm, build low-income housing as part of their Copley Square Air Rights proposal. Salloway reports that "video brought unique capabilities to the group discussion process such as compression of time events, the ability to allow viewers to witness interactions and present relationships they were not likely to see." The use of the tapes by people involved in the actual events led the MIT staff to conclude that "telecommunications can reverse the 'trickle down' relationship in which citizens are on the receiving end of public policy outcomes. Visual productions like 'Copley Square' have the power to shape public debate and to create a platform for public consensus." Once completed, the taped report was filed in the Laboratory of Architecture and Planning for later use by students.

Design: Case Studies

Case study is common in business and law education. Since 1964, a growing group of engineering educators has worked to make the case studies method a valuable part of engineering instruction (e.g., Vesper and Adams, 1969; 1971). Today, the headquarters of the American Society for Engineering Education (ASEE) publishes an annual catalog containing about 270 documented and reviewed cases which are available for a nominal charge. About 100 orders are filled annually. A total of 988 individual cases were distributed last year; the most popular dozen cases were requested 10 to 14 times. Almost without exception, the cases are typed manuscripts which are reproduced on demand. Though protected by copyright, permission to copy cases locally is routinely given.

Role of ITV: In a quite separate activity, the Open University of the United Kingdom has demonstrated how TV can add an important dimension to case studies. The Open University prepares coordinated sets of materials built primarily around a paperback textbook, but these are supplemented by both audiotapes and videotapes. Two excellent examples (from a rather short list of interest to engineers) are the courses on "Systems Performance: Human Factors and Systems" and "Systems Modelling." Case studies, produced by the British Broadcasting Company (BBC) on audiotapes and videotapes, are interspersed throughout the course. Note that not only do the cases provide motivating interludes to consolidate learning, they also offer specific examples of both the applications and the limitations of theory.

ITV offers the instructor an important complementary tool in the case study approach to engineering education, but the resources required if ITV is to have a significant impact are not yet available. Indeed, the Open University material appears to be the only available in engineering education to date.

Professional Ethics: Instruction in professional ethics for engineers is being encouraged anew. The U.S. accreditation society, Engineer's Council for Professional Development/Accreditation Board for Engineering and Technology (ECPD/ABET), devoted much of its 1977 Annual Meeting to this topic. Team teaching approaches, which usually involve philosophy and engineering instructors, are gaining favor. Much, much more needs to be done in this area; it has been neglected for a decade.

One powerful example from medical education is cited to illustrate the potential of media in instruction in professional ethics. "Who Should Survive" is a 26-minute film from the Joseph P. Kennedy, Jr. Foundation (Film Service, 999 Asylum Avenue, Hartford, Connecticut). The case described is an adaptation of an actual case that occurred at the Johns Hopkins Hospital; the staff play their real life roles. A mongoloid child is born with an intestinal block which can be cured only by an operation. The parents do not want the burden of a retarded child and refuse to permit the operation. The surgeon and hospital do not challenge the decision in the courts. In 15 days, the infant dies. A panel of five persons (a mother, a physician, a priest, a law professor, and a sociology professor) discusses the ethical, legal, and scientific issues involved. The viewer is left with a set of provocative questions. Did this helpless infant have to die? Did the doctors and the hospital have to accede to the parents' refusal to permit a simple operation? Was there no appeal to higher authority? Who decides who should survive? The film is acclaimed as an outstanding instructional tool. A brief printed enclosure is provided to help stimulate and guide discussion; it also provides a list of suggested readings.

Engineers also face ethical dilemmas in complex situations that often involve human safety and well-being. Production of films presenting case studies similar to the one described above would be an excellent project for foundations to underwrite. The American Bar Association has a modest effort underway for lawyers (Hamblin, 1978). Although no comparable films exist on ethical issues in engineering practice, The American Society for Civil Engineers has begun circulating to student chapters an hour-and-a-half videotape which focuses on the procedures that society follows in reaching decisions on ethical complaints. Also, a clearinghouse for materials, such as course outlines and reading lists, has been established at Rensselaer Polytechnic Institute for instructors in professional ethics for engineers. In addition, the National Science Foundation's Science Education Directorate sponsors a very modest set of projects that are primarily aimed at documentation.

Interviews/Career Guidance

Engineering education usually neglects the rich human history of the profession. Young people today show more interest than their recent predecessors in the values and personalities of engineers in practice. Florman's book, The Existential Pleasures of Engineering (1975), is a reflection of this concern. Television might play a unique role in bringing life to a curriculum overburdened with abstract analysis.

The Bell Laboratories are now producing a documentary television series which they call "Communications Milestones." These are brief, informal visits with engineers and scientists who have made outstanding contributions. They describe the setting for their discovery, the work which led to the concept or invention, and the reaction of their peers and the profession in the United States and abroad. One of the most interesting features in each tape is the insight provided by the individual inventor about his own experience with the creative process (Feinstein, 1978).

Business educators have created a clearinghouse to encourage the development and distribution of video documentaries with the support of a private foundation. The objective is to videotape interviews with contemporary business leaders in their areas of expertise. The material has many uses. For example, a workshop for educators was held in 1977 at CSU where the files are maintained.

Ellison Smith (1974) discusses the use of TV and radio to assist engineering colleges in influencing high school students in making career decisions. Examples range from radio spots with popular disc jockeys to films aimed at minorities and women.

John Truxal and Ludwig Braun created the National Coordinating Center for Curriculum Development at SUNY-Stony Brook to increase the number of minority students who chose to study engineering. Working with young people in grades 9 through 12, they provide resource material to schools in Chicago, New York City, Atlanta, Rochester, Buffalo, and California (MESA Program). Films prepared by industry to interest minority students in engineering careers are proving to be effective motivational resources. The use of calculators and personal computers as a part of this program is described later in this report.

The most popular films shown on the freshman dormitory CATV at CSU deal with career guidance. Many freshmen are uncertain about a specific major and the variety of work available upon graduation. Unfortunately, many of the films available from government agencies and technical societies are heroic rather than realistic in portraying the work of engineers. The ASEE Annual Meeting usually sponsors a "film fair" where these materials may be viewed and discussed.

Applications to Engineering Education Off Campus

Off-campus applications clearly surpass all other uses of ITV in engineering education. Since the mid-1960's, over 30 major colleges of engineering have developed regional ITV systems to deliver both graduate and continuing education to engineers at their job sites. Recently, 22 of these universities have formed a consortium to extend these services nationwide. Other examples of ITV used to link colleges of engineering with junior colleges, high schools, and foreign universities show considerable promise but are rare.

Graduate Education

The Goals of Engineering Education report in 1968 (Pettit and Hawkins, 1968) recognized the need for developing "on-campus study programs for employees of nearby industry and government laboratories," as well as for continued experimentation in "extending high quality advanced-degree education to engineering students employed at locations remote from established campuses." This recommendation has been widely supported in the engineering academic community, and it has been implemented primarily through the use of ITV systems. Early experiments with leased microwave links for an occasional class have evolved into large operational programs using a variety of dedicated delivery systems throughout the year.

Table 1 lists the academic credit video-based engineering graduate programs by originating university and provides the following information: program starting date; delivery method; number of remote locations served; number of engineering courses; total enrollments off campus; and an indication of whether graduate business courses are offered in conjunction with engineering courses in the delivery system. These data were collected specifically for this paper; any omissions should be reported to the authors.

The graduate courses are regularly scheduled on-campus offerings which are attended by full-time students. The classes are held in specially equipped studio classrooms so that not only the lectures but also the student questions and discussions are transmitted. To convert a regular classroom for video origination, together with the usual control equipment, costs from $25,000 to $35,000 (Miller and Baldwin, 1975).

Although the studio-classrooms are similar, a variety of signal delivery systems are employed to link the graduate students at job sites to the campus. The first major system, established in 1964 at the University of Florida, employed two-way, point-to-point microwave which was leased from the telephone company to link the main campus to several extension centers in central Florida. In 1969, Stanford University began serving in-plant classrooms in the San Francisco Bay Area with a four-channel instructional television fixed service (ITFS) system that featured FM-talkback capability. In 1967, CSU was the first to employ courier-carried videotape as a delivery system; tapes are returned, erased, and reused on a schedule. Today, most microwave and ITFS receiving sites are equipped with video recorders to store the instruction temporarily either for review or for making up missed classes. By scheduling occasional visits and regular office hours for telephone consultations, faculty employing videotape in regional systems have largely overcome the talkback disadvantage of videotape delivery. The convenience of decoupling the campus and part-time student schedules is, of course, a major advantage of videotape. Newer systems tend to employ combinations of delivery methods to fit the needs of specific geographic areas.

A study of the ITV operations at Stanford, University of California at Davis, and CSU showed that the dominant cost in all three systems is administrative program management and technical manpower to run the

TABLE 1
ACADEMIC CREDIT
ENGINEERING GRADUATE PROGRAMS OFFERED OFF CAMPUS BY TELEVISION
1979-80

Program (Starting Date)	Delivery Method	Remote Locations	Total Courses	Total Enrollments	Graduate Business Courses Also
University of Rhode Island (1961)	Microwave	Discontinued 1979			No
University of Florida (1964)	Leased Microwave	Program Ended in 1972			No
Southern Methodist University-TAGER (1967)	Microwave + ITFS + Videotape	16	75	1152	No
Colorado State University (1967)	Videotape	37	76	900	Yes
University of Tennessee (1967)	Videotape	16	55	568	Ceased 80-81
University of Illinois/Urbana (1967)	Blackboard by Wire	4	22	140	No
University of Colorado (1968)	Videotape + ITFS	14	15	152	No
Stanford University (1969)	ITFS + Videotape	45	149	2373	No
ACE at Stanford (1969)	ITFS + Videotape	36	10	448	Yes
Iowa State University (1969)	Videotape	15	34	275	Yes
University of South Carolina (1969)	ITV + Videotape	33	51	2385	Yes
MIT (1969)	Videotape	Only Non-Credit Courses Offered			
University of Kentucky (1969)	Film + Videotape	Only Non-Credit Courses Offered			
University of Michigan (1970)	Leased Microwave + ITFS	11	46	311	Yes
University of California at Davis (1970)	Microwave + Videotape	3	47	320	No
Purdue University (1970)	Microwave + Videotape	15	12	166	No
University of Wisconsin (1970)	ETV+Videotape+Electrowriter+Telephone Network	NA	NA	7	No
University of Minnesota (1971)	Microwave + ITFS + Videotape	17	55	909	No
Rochester Institute of Technology (1971)	Videotape	NA	NA	NA	No
Oklahoma State System (1972)	Microwave & ITFS	NA	NA	NA	Yes
University of Maine (1972)	Live Video, Audio Return	Not Currently Operating			
Case Western Reserve (1972)	Videotape	50	41	326	Yes
University of Southern California (1972)	ITFS	27	92	785	No
University of Arizona (1972)	Videotape + Microwave(Out) + Slow Scan (Return)	20	47	97	Yes
University of Pennsylvania (1972)	ITFS	Not Currently Operating			
Cornell University (1973)	Videotape				
University of California/Santa Barbara (1974)	Microwave + Videotape	2	23	95	No
University of California/Berkeley (1974)	Microwave + Videotape	6	30	-	No
University of Idaho (1975)	Videotape	130	32	332	Yes
University of Massachusetts (1975)	Videotape	128	26	154	No
Illinois Institute of Technology (1976)	ITFS	18	114	780	Yes
North Carolina State University (1976)	Videotape	12	14	220	No
Georgia Institute of Technology (1978)	Videotape	10	18	105	Yes
Polytechnic Institute of New York (1978)	Videotape				
Worcester Polytechnic Institute	Videotape - In Planning				
University of Maryland	Beginning 1980-81				Yes
Auburn University	In Planning				

video technology (Loomis and Brandt, 1973). This factor accounts for $20 to $30 of a "total" cost of $30 to $50 per TV classroom-lecture-hour. Furthermore, another $4 to $7 per TV classroom-lecture-hour is required to outfit the TV classroom regardless of delivery mode. Audio talkback, if used, is surprisingly expensive, perhaps $1 to $7 per TV classroom-lecture-hour. In the total cost cited above, no provision to pay the instructor is included, the argument being that the instructor is simply adding off-campus students to a regularly scheduled class. Even with this drastic assumption of cost allocation, only one university (Stanford) has demonstrated full recovery of the incremental costs of its television delivery system (Morris, et al., 1974). It is important to note, however, that virtually all tuition and other direct charges are paid by the employer in every system.

It should be no surprise that regular campus classes appeal primarily to the young engineering employees. Several universities listed in Table 1 report that only 5 to 15 percent of the off-campus course enrollees for credit are engineers over 35 years of age (Schmaling, 1974). Often, about a third of the participants in these credit programs are pursuing a program of study leading to a M.S. degree. The cumulative degrees awarded to date to ITV students at their job sites is summarized in Table 2.

Federal government grants were not a significant factor in the development of any of the systems listed in Table 1. User subscriptions to a capital fund, private foundation donations, and state and university funds built the systems. The engineering outreach programs are a local, grassroots response to a professional need.

The ITV programs are very effective and popular with the mature, goal-oriented engineers who elect to participate. Convenience is often cited as motivating factor: "time saved in travel to class"; "only way available"; "can make up classes missed while on business travel"; "fits my work schedule" (Neidt and Baldwin, 1970; Stutzman and Grigsby, 1973; Down, 1976). The average performance of off-campus students is usually quite close to that of the on-campus students when comparable admission criteria are employed. R. M. Anderson, Jr. reports on evaluations of 1,500 students enrolled in 60 ITV courses at Purdue University using a variety of delivery modes both on and off campus:

> The data indicate that students do learn by televised
> instruction, that students prefer TV-with-audio-talkback
> over videotaped instruction, and that students prefer live
> instruction to either kind of televised instruction.
> (Anderson, 1978)

The results above pool both on-campus and off-campus student attitudes.

Rogers (1978) compares the broadcast mode with videotape delivery based on the experience at Case Western Reserve University. He concludes:

> While each case must be decided on its own merits, our
> member companies have opted for videotape, largely on the
> basis of its scheduling convenience and flexibility.
> (Rogers, 1978)

TABLE 2

GRADUATE PROGRAMS OFFERED OFF CAMPUS BY TELEVISION

MS Engineering/MBA Degrees Awarded to Date

University of Rhode Island	NA
University of Florida	253
Southern Methodist University-TAGER	331
Colorado State University	165
University of Tennessee	114
University of Illinois/Urbana	NA
University of Colorado	2
Stanford University	245
ACE at Stanford	170
Iowa State University	10
University of South Carolina	375
University of Michigan	160
University of California at Davis	50
Purdue University	183
University of California/Santa Barbara	82
University of Minnesota	55
Oklahoma State System	NA
Rochester Institute of Technology	51
Case Western Reserve University	40
University of Southern California	525
University of Arizona	11
Cornell University	4
University of Idaho	10
University of Massachusetts	1

(11/80)

Gibbons, et al. (1977) report on the use of videotaped instruction which is supported by local tutors drawn from the engineering staff of the industrial sponsor. Data are presented that show that the part-time students in industry can significantly out-perform campus students with comparable academic records in the same course.

Very little systematic research has been undertaken to determine the relative importance of various courseware and environmental variables in the video-based instruction of adult professionals. The operating systems are large enough and sufficiently dispersed to enable statistical studies to be designed, but external funds and specialists not now involved in these operations are necessary to undertake such work. Moreover, the operating systems themselves could not support such studies from existing revenues.

The ITV invasion of the job site has benefited not only the

participating students, but it also has benefited the engineering
faculty who find regular interaction with the industrial students
stimulating and professionally rewarding. Figure 4 shows the steady
growth of these off-campus graduate and continuing education programs
nationally. The enrollment data provided include the non-credit,
continuing education application of ITV as discussed in the next
section. Non-credit offerings are currently the most rapidly growing
segment of off-campus ITV in engineering education.

A number of unresolved problems are worth noting however. Most of
the programs are regional and employ a courier to carry hardcopy to and
from campus. An important element in the increased productivity of
faculty in these programs is the ability to keep all student groups on
a reasonably close schedule. Otherwise, a faculty member actually
teaches many different courses rather than different sections of the
same course. At long distances, say over 100 miles, maintaining a
schedule can be very difficult, though both the University of Arizona
and Stanford University have experimented with videotaped credit
courses at distant sites. New communications technologies promise to
help overcome the regionalism which dominates these systems today.

Continuing Education

A relatively stable population of engineers is increasingly
involved with the development of new technologies and with changing
societal attitudes toward technology. Recent studies (e.g., Alden,
1974 and Seltzer, 1975, 1976) place the engineering workforce at over a
million people. Nearly all of these are men and many are without
college degrees in engineering. One of the difficulties in coping with
change is the relatively slow growth of the profession. The median age
is 43, and the rate of entry of new graduates into the field of
engineering today barely exceeds the rate of departure through death,
retirement, or change of occupation. Concern arising from charges of
age-discriminatory practices has prompted the enlargement of continuing
education opportunities in some firms and agencies (e.g., Rivers, 1975
and C&E News, 1975).

Participants in continuing education courses usually differ in age
and motivation from part-time graduate students. Academic credit is
much less important, though some recognition or certification is often
desired. Professional development per se is often cited as a dominant
motivation: "keeping up to date"; "useful in job"; "self-improvement";
"learning new skills." Down (1976) reports that auditors in the
Stanford ITV system have an average age of 38.1 years, compared with
27.9 for the engineers who take the courses for credit.

In addition to allowing auditors in regular graduate classes,
special curricula are developed to serve the continuing education needs
of engineers in the Stanford system by the Association for Continuing
Education (ACE). This non-profit organization is a unique regional
consortium of universities and employers of engineers (Davis and
Gunderson, 1974). It also uses the Stanford ITFS delivery system. A
wide variety of courses is offered by ACE. Instructors drawn from
industry rarely teach these courses, though this was part of the

34

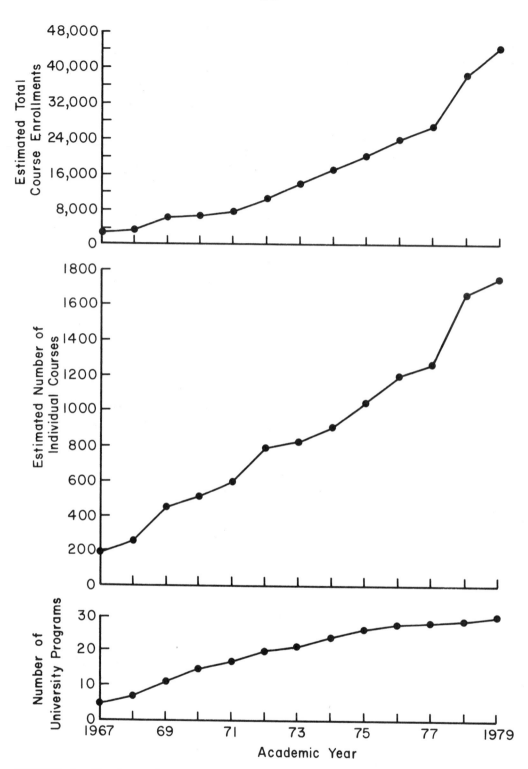

FIGURE 4 Engineering graduate and continuing education programs
offered off campus by television.

original rationale for forming ACE. The continuing education offerings generally are scheduled after regular working hours, and, apparently, some companies have enough red tape to discourage potential instructors. ACE courses usually are taught in the candid classroom mode during hours when Stanford does not schedule other programming, e.g., early morning, noon, late afternoon, and evening.

The Center for Advanced Engineering Study (CAES) at MIT pioneered the development of continuing education packages. These modular courses consist of a coordinated set of videotaped lectures/ demonstrations, study guides that include all of the visual aids used in the lectures, problem sets with solutions, textbooks, and, occasionally, computer decks and manuals. The average length of a course is 12 to 15 lectures, each about 30 minutes long. The content is oriented to practicing engineers, not young graduate students. The videotapes are produced in a color studio with the benefit of special graphics and highlighting techniques. The materials so produced are available at any time of the year, since, unlike the classroom tapes described earlier, the intention here is to create a master tape for later reproduction or videopublishing. Distribution is an expensive, frustrating feature of videopublishing today. Indeed, MIT-CAES was not able to meet expenses during any year from the inception of the program to 1975. This program has continued to grow steadily, become self-supporting, and now is the largest effort of its kind in the world.

Perhaps this explains why only a few universities have produced more than one subject in this packaged format. The University of Wisconsin Extension has four video-based courses in engineering with specially designed textual materials. Rochester Institute of Technology has produced 10 courses in a studio for national distribution. ACE has developed several topics, and CSU has 22 short courses which were prepared in its color studio. Overall though, videopublishing for engineering continuing education in campus studios is in its infancy.

Other non-university organizations have produced video-based courseware for the use of practicing engineers. Commercially, the most notable are: Advanced Systems, Inc., which lists over 50 multi-media courses, varying from three to ten video sessions each, in management and electronic data processing; Texas Instruments, which lists over 10 multi-media courses of about 10 sessions each on solid state electronic technology; and Hewlett Packard, which lists over 160 topics in electronics and in the operation and maintenance of a wide range of specific equipment. Many other firms have employed video-based instruction for in-service training, and companies such as IBM and Bell Telephone Laboratories have modest catalogs covering a variety of subject matter. However, with the exception of the Advanced Systems, Texas Instruments, and Hewlett Packard courseware, there is little sharing of such materials across company lines.

The activities of technical societies in media-based continuing education for professionals was the subject of a conference in 1977 (Lykos, 1978a). The American Chemical Society (ACS) reported on the use of 5 ACS videotaped short courses and 37 audiotaped short courses, all with coordinated printed material. The ACS is currently engaged in an evaluation of individually controlled, media-augmented courses with the assistance of a $830,000 grant from NSF. This is slated for completion in 1981. The Society of Manufacturing Engineers reported on the development of a number of short courses and single-topic lectures for videotaped distribution. A representative of the American Medical Association discussed work underway to use a microprocessor controlled videodisc. However, most technical societies presented a very cautious approach to media, viewing ET as a costly and risky venture for self-supporting, continuing education groups to undertake.

At MIT, Project PROCEED (Program for Continuing Engineering Education) is relying primarily on printed material arranged in modular fashion for individual study. The design features include effective use of case studies as well as an elaborate adaptive reference system. Preliminary reports on this $770,000 effort, the only other large NSF activity in continuing education, are available (Cohen, 1977, 1978).

In an earlier development, representatives from all of the colleges of engineering known to have ITV systems in operation gathered in Dallas for a "Workshop on Continuing Education for Engineers at Midcareer" in August 1974. The 70 participants were drawn equally from industry and universities. Features of in-plant, video-based instruction which were viewed favorably in the discussions were summarized as follows:

> Participants from both industry and universities discussed the potential advantages of videotaped instruction which are not yet widely exploited in existing programs. For example, distribution can potentially be nationwide to spread the cost of curricula development and delivery over many learners. Files can be maintained at the discretion of the user. The "best" instructors can be contacted in a region or discipline area. Evaluation can lead to revision and improvement of specific segments of an instructional program. Live instructors drawn from the universities or student peer groups can adapt and supplement the video modules in much the same fashion that many university instructors now employ textbooks, at reasonable additional cost. Intensive short courses and longer study leaves are, of course, very effective continuing educational activities, but, because of the time away from the job, only a small percentage of the engineers have an opportunity to participate. Indeed, the rarity makes it something of a reward for good service in some firms or a transition signal of a promotion. Video instruction in the place of employment at a reasonable cost offers the real potential of serving many engineers. (Baldwin, et al., 1974)

Some of the shortcomings of these early efforts were also listed:

> Among the factors which were identified as contributing to this poor result are: university courses are graduate offerings in engineering which require more skill in

mathematics than the older engineer possesses; fear of
competition for grades with younger engineers; lack of
relevance of coursework to job; job related incentives are
lacking and indeed may actively work against the older
engineer seeking credit or a degree from a university;
family pressures which compete with study time off the
job. Coursework has not been designed which correlates
well with the professional growth of engineers, either as
technical specialists or as managers. Some participants
felt strongly that up-dating of technical skills had been
over-emphasized (who wants to admit that he is outdated?),
and that even MBA programs, where available, are not well
designed for engineers seeking management positions.
(ibid.)

Tribus (1975) argues that more attention must be paid in continuing
education to the way industry usually organizes engineering work into
specific functions such as designing, manufacturing, and evaluating.
These activities draw on a variety of traditional engineering
disciplines in ways which are often unique to an industry.

A number of planning sessions followed the 1974 Dallas workshop in
which sets of mutual objectives were identified and an organizational
structure formulated. In April 1976, twelve university representatives
formally created a non-profit corporation called the Association for
Media-Based Continuing Education for Engineers (AMCEE). This
consortium of universities that operates ITV systems sets out its
goal: To increase the national effectiveness of continuing education
of engineers. The member institutions today are:

TABLE 3
AMCEE MEMBER INSTITUTIONS

Auburn University	University of Arizona
Case Western Reserve University	University of California/Davis
Colorado State University	University of Idaho
Georgia Institute of Technology	University of Illinois, Urbana-Champaign
Illinois Institute of Technology	University of Kentucky
Massachusetts Institute of Tech.	University of Maryland
North Carolina State University	University of Massachusetts/Amherst
Polytechnic Institute of New York	University of Michigan
Purdue University	University of Minnesota
Southern Methodist University	University of South Carolina
Stanford University	University of Southern California

Before AMCEE, these schools were independently offering
television-based courses at the graduate level to
on-the-job engineers at their place of work but were
drawing only on their separate faculties to develop and
teach such courses. This was a wasteful non-system of

providing for a homogeneous group of people with a real
need for, and a strong interest in, advanced education,
and it prevented the offering of specialized courses for
which there was a demand but no expertise in the local
faculty.

The obvious solution was some kind of cooperative
organization that could sponsor the development of
courses and other materials for use by all the schools
involved, that could share development costs among the
schools, and that could afford to offer highly
specialized courses that might have only a few students
at a given site but a substantial number throughout the
consortium. AMCEE expects its membership to grow to
twenty-five or more institutions in the next few years
and expects to expand its offerings to laboratory
technicians and other people besides engineers working in
technical jobs. AMCEE uses a revolving fund from which
awards are made on a competitive basis for the
development of new courses, and this venture capital will
be returned to the fund as new courses are brought by the
members of the consortium and by other institutions.
Whether a similar consortium might be appropriate in
other large professional fields such as medicine,
nursing, law, management, and public school teaching is a
question that should now be explored. (Koerner, 1977)

The Sloan Foundation and NSF have provided funds to launch a
coordinated set of activities which addresses both the goal of the
organization and the long-term need for AMCEE to be self-sufficient by
virtue of the sale of its services. AMCEE produced a catalog of 172
courses from 10 universities in July 1978; the October edition listed
224 courses from 15 universities. The 1979/80 AMCEE catalog listed
over 350 courses from 15 universities; by 1980/81, over 450 courses
from 21 universities appeared. For the first time, university ITV
courses are available from a single source nationwide.

Several special workshops and seminars on timely topics of interest
to engineers have been held; each drew on talent from several colleges
for faculty. A biannual directory of all continuing education
opportunities for engineers plus a telephone information service
supported by a word processor are scheduled for introduction in late
1980. AMCEE sponsored the conference cited earlier (Lykos, 1978a) at
the United Engineering Center, New York City, September 28-29, 1978.
This meeting brought together representatives of many major technical
societies and universities to discuss ways to cooperate in the use of
media in continuing education. AMCEE also sponsored a feasibility
study on the possible use of modern communications technology and
satellites as discussed in Chapter III.

Videopublishing received a boost three years ago when the
University of Southern California (USC) started its Employee
Development Program. Courses produced at other institutions are

previewed on the USC ITV system periodically. Those drawing sufficient response are scheduled for distribution over the system on a non-credit basis. Enrollments in these non-credit courses now exceeds that of the regular credit offerings. AMCEE has encouraged similar successful programs at the University of South Carolina, the University of Michigan, Purdue, and CSU.

An evaluation of the CSU program showed that the off-campus students were not concerned about where the course was prepared. Rather, they focused on the relevance and quality of the instruction (Sjogren, 1976). Table 4 summarizes the non-credit program enrollment for 1979-80. The regional ITV systems promise to be effective distributers in the videopublishing field. In addition, the regional ITV systems often supply the advising, tutoring, and quality control functions needed by the industrial subscribers. As previously noted, these non-credit programs are the most rapidly growing segment of ITV instruction.

Evaluations of continuing education programs are customarily limited to attitude surveys of the participants. Employers usually express faith in the long-term benefits and do not fret over evaluations (Sanders, 1974). Morris (1978) reports on an NSF-sponsored study which attempts to measure the return on investment in continuing education of engineers. Detailed data on approximately 400 individuals in three firms and a government research laboratory were coded for 5 to 15 years of employment records. In addition to continuing education participation, other characteristics of the individual were coded such as quality of performance on the job, college stature and college grade point average, honors, and personal drive. Morris reports "a convincing statistical association between continuing education and performance, and a demonstration that it is not a false association created by any other variable which was measured." In a less ambitious study, Klus and Jones (1975) reported that "participation in continuing education programs (in this case, short, live courses) seems to have a positive effect on those job factors pertaining to salary and satisfaction with present job status."

Some of the current impediments to the use of ITV at the job site for continuing education include:

- Lack of a well-accepted credentialing method (the CEU or continuing education unit draws mixed responses);
- Lack of curriculum depth; and
- Inefficient distribution economics for materials designed for continuing education.

Junior Colleges

Resource sharing is particularly attractive when budgets are lean in higher education. The rapid expansion of junior colleges during the late 1960's left many state university systems with tight budgets. Many junior colleges were poorly funded from the outset, yet colleges of engineering increasingly are asked to assimilate transfer students

TABLE 4
NON-ACADEMIC CREDIT
ENGINEERING CONTINUING EDUCATION PROGRAMS OFFERED OFF CAMPUS BY TELEVISION
1979-80

Program (Starting Date)	Delivery Method	Remote Locations	Total Courses	Total Enrollments
University of Rhode Island (1961)	Microwave	Program Discontinued 1979		
University of Florida (1964)	Leased Microwave	Program Discontinued 1972		
Southern Methodist University-TAGER (1967)	Microwave + ITFS + Videotape	16	75	60
Colorado State University (1967)	Videotape	525	24	2934
University of Tennessee (1967)	Videotape	All Credit Courses Offered		
University of Illinois/Urbana (1967)	Blackboard by Wire	4	22	16
University of Colorado (1968)	Videotape + ITFS	11	5	121
Stanford University (1969)	ITFS + Videotape	45	149	1655
ACE at Stanford (1969)	ITFS + Videotape	36	68	3615
Iowa State University (1969)	Videotape	NA	1	826
University of South Carolina (1969)	ITV + Videotape	All Credit Courses Offered		
MIT (1969)	Videotape	800	24	15,000
University of Kentucky (1969)	Film + Videotape	29	2	910
University of Michigan (1970)	Leased Microwave + ITFS	11	46	352
University of California at Davis (1970)	Microwave + Videotape	3	47	103
Purdue University (1970)	Microwave + Videotape	13	17	688
North Carolina State University (1970)	ETV + Videotape	30	11	706
University of Wisconsin (1970)	ETV+Videotape+Electrowriter+Telephone Network	NA	30	1289
University of Minnesota (1971)	Microwave + ITFS + Videotape	All Credit Courses Offered		
Rochester Institute of Technology (1971)	Videotape			
Oklahoma State System (1972)	Microwave + ITFS	All Credit Courses Offered		
University of Maine (1972)	Live Video, Audio Return	Not Currently Operating		
Case Western Reserve (1972)	Videotape	50	41	14
University of Southern California (1972)	ITFS	27	153	2798
University of Arizona (1972)	Videotape + Microwave(Out) + Slow Scan (Return)	60	44	NA
University of Pennsylvania (1972)	ITFS	Not Currently Operating		
Cornell University (1973)	Videotape			
University of California/Santa Barbara (1974)	Microwave + Videotape	All Credit Courses Offered		
University of California/Berkeley (1974)	Microwave + Videotape	6	30	250
University of Idaho (1975)	Videotape	20	8	209
University of Massachusetts (1975)	Videotape	8	7	175
Illinois Institute of Technology (1976)	ITFS	7	7	114
Georgia Institute of Technology (1978)	Videotape	All Credit Courses Offered		
Polytechnic Institute of New York (1978)	Videotape			
Worcester Polytechnic Institute	Videotape - In Planning			
University of Maryland	Beginning 1980-81			
Auburn University	In Planning			

who have two years of study in junior colleges. Project Co-Tie, which began in 1968, seeks to achieve increased and enhanced educational opportunities by means of resource sharing among Colorado junior colleges and CSU.

> Since its beginning Co-Tie has included, among its activities, the offering of pre-engineering courses to participating colleges. Electrical Circuits, Statics, Dynamics, Fluids, and Thermal Sciences are common core pre-engineering courses which have been videotaped for use in the program. Six of the participating colleges offered two-year pre-engineering programs; however, each of the programs had notable differences primarily in the sophomore engineering courses. The Co-Tie project supplemented each of the pre-engineering programs to the extent that a student could transfer into a four-year program as a full-fledged junior. The videotaped courses are made available free of charge to the colleges to use in a manner dictated by local faculty. Each of the colleges charges its own tuition and awards its own credit for the courses even though the material is identical to that offered at Colorado State University. (Maxwell, 1978)

An important feature of Co-Tie is a state-owned data and voice communications network which links nine campuses to the CSU digital computer. Prior to this development in 1971, many junior colleges in Colorado were essentially without computing facilities for student use.

For years, some students have chosen to start their collegiate educations at small liberal arts colleges. Often, transfer arrangements are offered so that the student first attends the smaller college for three years and then transfers to a specified engineering college for two additional years of study. Successful completion of a three-two program results in the awarding of a B.A. degree usually in mathematics or science from the liberal arts college and a B.S. degree in engineering. The Illinois Institute of Technology recently entered into an arrangement with North Central College which is within the 35-mile radius of its ITFS system, IIT/V. Coordination of programs is enhanced through joint seminars so that students can enlarge their selection of courses before transferring.

High Schools

Many of Colorado's smaller and relatively remote rural high schools simply are unable to offer a complete set of pre-college mathematics courses because of the small numbers of students involved. While relatively large metropolitan high schools offer a wide range of required as well as elective mathematics, science, and computing courses, the curricula are "barebones" in most rural schools. For example, virtually no rural high school in Colorado has its own computing facility and offers computing classes.

In order to extend high school engineering programs and to provide some assistance to rural high schools, the Hi-Tie program was established in 1971. Through Hi-Tie, CSU has offered its freshman engineering course via videotape to senior students at any high school wishing to participate for the past nine years. During the 1979-80 academic year, approximately 25 students at 6 high schools earned university credit by taking the CSU freshman engineering course. The videotaped course covers basic Fortran IV programming and its engineering applications. In addition, five one-credit precalculus mathematics courses and a university mathematics placement examination are being offered to 50 students in 8 high schools. Taping is done in a studio-classroom with one section of CSU freshman engineering students.

Special sessions are included in the video series relating to "what engineering is all about." A number of campus groups such as the Institute of Electrical and Electronics Engineers student chapter and the Society for Women Engineers have made short videotape segments. Other segments address career opportunities and the life of the working engineer. The segments are edited onto the end of shortened lectures and are used as the advertisement of the day. Produced mostly by students, these special spots are effective in depicting the campus life of an undergraduate engineer to high school students. The high school students view the course tapes made at CSU on a regularly scheduled basis (Ward and Maxwell, 1975).

Programs such as these might well serve as an effective communications link between minority students attending high schools and universities. Because researchers often believe that high school is too late, other ways of supporting science and mathematics instruction in junior high schools and earlier need to be found as well.

Public Understanding of Technology

The NOVA television series shown over the Public Broadcasting System (PBS) is the best known and most long-lived example of programs designed to promote public understanding of technology. A new series produced with support from NSF and General Motors Research Laboratories is called "How about..." and features Don Herbert. (Herbert is known to most as "Mr. Wizard" from an earlier series.) "How about..." is produced in 90-second segments intended to be used in local news programming and "aimed at adult viewers who want to know more about how science and technology affect their lives - present and future." During 1978-79, 65 segments were produced, ranging over a wide variety of topics such as: "Mount Rainer, the Sleeping Volcano"; "3-D Pictures of Holography"; "Inside a Hand-Held Calculator"; "The Radar-Gun that Clocks Your Speed': and "Listening for Space Signals." The series first appeared in 1980 on 138 commercial television stations.

New technology can be very threatening in an established organization. Consider the general morale problems which might be encountered in the automobile industry as microelectronics is introduced. Assuming that the engineers can quickly assimilate the new technology through on-the-job training, what can be done to gain the understanding and approval of the support staff of the organization? General Motors/Delco Division purchased the introductory courses produced by Texas Instruments which describe solid state devices and give an overview of microelectronics. These video lectures are shown in the plant at various times. Everyone, e.g., secretaries, clerks, janitors, is encouraged to participate so that the new activities of the division can be better understood, and perhaps supported, by all (Holmes, 1978).

Foreign Programs

Many engineering colleges have participated in programs which involve assistance to foreign universities or various kinds of technical planning and development work for foreign governments. The activities of the International Division of ASEE attest to this commitment abroad. Clearly, many engineering faculty willingly devote several years of their careers to overseas work on the wide variety of activities required by foreign contracts. The faculty's personal encounters and experiences are probably essential. The extent to which ITV or other media can be used to enlarge the talent and resources devoted to such programs is an issue.

The University of Catania in southern Italy contracted with CSU to produce a course entitled "Management of Water Resource Systems: A Systems Approach." A team of faculty from each university developed the course outline, and eight CSU faculty shared in scripting the 30 hours of videotape and the companion text. The media production employs voice over a sequence of prepared graphics, film, and slides to illustrate the topic. An instructor does not appear on camera at any time. Sound tracks in both English and Italian were recorded on the original tapes; these have since been translated into two other languages as well. The course was finished in 1976, after two years of effort, and is now in use both on the campus of the University of Catania and in various government agencies in the arid regions of Italy (Baldwin and Davis, 1975).

Rogers (1975) reports on the development of a 40-hour program of technical training for use at Kam AZ, a gigantic automotive factory built with U.S. equipment on the Kama River in the Soviet Union. The C-E Cast Equipment Division of W.S. Tyler, Inc., contracted to deliver seven automatic molding lines for the sand casting of engine blocks and other parts to this factory. Each line is a hugh machine, approximately 200 feet in length, composed of mechanical, pneumatic, hydraulic, electrical, and electronic sub-systems. The U.S. contractor promised to supply instruction in the principles, operation, and maintenance of the devices. In the United States, this would be accomplished by presentations made by representatives of over 20 component suppliers, as well as the C-E Cast Equipment staff. A variety of slide sets, film strips, videotapes, working models, drawings, and catalogs would be used. Because of time and funding constraints, the decision was made to videotape each of these presentations in the ITV classrooms of Case Western Reserve University so that the entire series would be in a common, storable format. Both English and Russian sound tracks accompany the training course, which has been used both on this contract and in the United States. Rogers reports that about 4.5 hours of production time were devoted to each hour of instruction, which is remarkable considering the lack of experience of the 29 instructors.

Two on-going activities related to public health and irrigation water management have taken CSU faculty teams to Egypt and Peru. In each case, training of native technicians is an important part of the project. Videotaped courses from campus provide an academic supplement to the field training being carried out by the CSU staff abroad. The task of selecting the most able natives for additional education in the United States is eased by noting performances on the taped graduate courses, and the transition into American graduate school is less traumatic for the students selected for further education.

But, reliable, fast communications systems are necessary if the resources of U.S. campuses are to have a major impact on the foreign assistance activities of engineering and agricultural faculties. Two-way interaction is essential. Several multinational industrial corporations now routinely employ satellite teleconferencing to improve the coordination of widely dispersed activities. Satellites offer an unparallelled opportunity which has yet to be exploited in the education of professionals in their homelands.

III.

NEW TECHNOLOGIES

The "new" technologies discussed in this Chapter are recent
applications of educational technology (ET) in engineering education.
Modern communications on a large geographic scale by satellite has
great potential as a logical extension of existing instructional
television (ITV) programs. Several experiments and feasibility
studies support this assertion. Secondly, advances in video
technology coupled with powerful decentralization computing may make a
new generation of instructional equipment affordable. This
possibility offers great opportunities to engineering education,
possibilities which are only now receiving serious study.

Satellite Applications and Potential

Engineering educators are pioneers in using media-based systems to
provide educational programs for their employed professional
constituents. In a recent study of continuing professional education
in law, medicine, teaching, and engineering, the engineering
profession was rated as "most promising as a market for electronic
delivery of continuing professional education." It also was pointed
out that "aside from their primary qualification as educational
institutions, universities are 'neutral' organizations within a
region, able to gain electronic entrance to, and disseminate
information among, many corporations and thus precipitate an
information flow which otherwise might not exist among competitors."
(Rothenberg, 1975)

A communications satellite which is placed in geostationary orbit
above the equator can provide broadcast coverage over about one-third
of the surface of the earth. Thus, it is possible to expand
educational television, radio, and data services from local or
regional coverage to national or international coverage. The
aggregation of large user groups receiving programming simultaneously
leads to a delivery cost per viewer that is reasonable when compared
with other communications options such as traveling to the point of
program origin or mailing film or videotape.

45

Through the Association for Media-Based Continuing Education for Engineers (AMCEE), the engineering educators who pioneered the use of media-based programs for practicing engineers are actively studying all of the facets of using communications satellites to expand the number of courses and services to an even larger audience spread over a vast geographical area. The goal is to improve the quality of engineering education for the hundreds of thousands of engineers and scientists not presently receiving continuing education on a regular basis, while keeping cost at a level that is considered reasonable by both suppliers and users.

Current Status

The systems operating today fall into two major categories: 1) live transmission of courses from classrooms to companies over instructional television fixed service (ITFS) channels or over educational television (ETV) channels; and 2) mailed videotapes of either live or studio-produced instruction.

An ITFS signal has a broadcast range of about 30 miles. In areas such as Los Angeles or San Francisco, ITFS works well. Many high technology firms are located within range of the University of Southern California and Stanford University systems. In Colorado, however, because the terrain makes live broadcast impractical, Colorado State University (CSU) has built its off-campus program around a videotape distribution service. The Massachusetts Institute of Technology (MIT) has a program primarily based on a catalog of studio-produced engineering and science courses, and it depends on mail and parcel delivery services for worldwide distribution. Demand for certain of MIT's packaged courses is so high that, in one case, 20 complete sets of 21 tapes each are needed to meet circulation requirements. This alone represents an inventory investment of $15,000 to $20,000. The new tutored videotape instruction (TVI) program at Stanford permits students at locations remote from the campus to earn degree credit by viewing videotapes of Stanford lectures (Gibbons, et al., 1977). In the absence of the course instructors, tutors provided by participating companies assist students. The most troublesome aspect of this program is the slow delivery of homework and examinations to the Stanford professors. A minimum lag-time of one week must be built into the program to ensure stability in the viewing schedules at the remote sites.

These systems, while effective in reaching the well-defined constituencies of the producing universities, are generally unable to expand their services for the following reasons: technical, i.e., the signal can travel only a short distance for a reasonable cost; logistical, i.e., the mail and other delivery services are slow; and financial, i.e., a videotape inventory is expensive.

Because of its broad footprint, a communications satellite is capable of providing service which is effectively responsive to the technical, logistical, and financial constraints mentioned above. A signal can be transmitted from any single point to many receivers across the country without regard for distance or geographical barriers. The signal can be received simultaneously at all points in the system. Thus, given an aggregated user group, the cost per viewer of distribution can be substantially reduced.

Previous Experiments

The Educational Satellite Communications Demonstration was the first substantial federal investment in finding educational applications for communications satellites. Sponsored jointly by the National Aeronautics and Space Administration (NASA) and the Department of Health, Education, and Welfare, a series of three projects was operated during the 1974-75 academic year using the NASA-developed ATS-6. Color television was distributed by this high-powered satellite to small antennas at rural schools and other, similar sites. The three regional projects included the Appalachian Educational Satellite Project conducted by the Appalachian Regional Commission, the Satellite Technology Demonstration conducted by the Federation of Rocky Mountain States, and the ESCD/Alaska conducted by the Alaska Governor's Office of Telecommunications. Between $18 and $34 million (depending on how much of the satellite and launch costs are included) was spent on these demonstrations. The Educational Policy Research Center of the Syracuse Research Corporation reported extensively on the results of these projects (Educational Policy Research Center, 1976).

During the 1976-77 academic year, Stanford University in California and Carleton University in Ottawa conducted a curriculum-sharing experiment using the Communications Technology Satellite, an experimental high-powered satellite co-sponsored by the United States and Canada. Three objectives were identified: 1) to demonstrate the ability to expand the scope of instruction by sharing classes between universities with different emphases and orientations; 2) to develop optimum class presentation and student/teacher interaction techniques for remote curriculum sharing; and 3) to develop, demonstrate, and evaluate a cost-effective, digital video compression system in conjunction with efficient channel coding and modulation.

The experiment was designed to take advantage of in-place equipment. Stanford had been operating its four-channel ITFS network since 1969, and Carleton had set up a "Wired City" laboratory containing an array of television-communications equipment. During the two-quarter experiment, four courses and one seminar were sent by Stanford and three courses were provided by Carleton. Sharon Strover of the Institute for Communication Research at Stanford reported:

> What does the Stanford-Carleton-NASA-Ames
> curriculum-sharing experiment mean for the larger
> contingent of satellite users and satellite watchers? Is
> it a promise for the future or just another "ho-hum" in
> educational technology? Our conclusion must be somewhere
> in between these poles. The digital video operated well,
> promising more efficient use of bandwidth in the future;

serious scheduling and accreditation problems were
avoided; students were by and large satisfied with the
courses; and the project sustained satisfactory
operations from October 1976 to March 1977.
Curriculum-sharing proved, at least in this case, not to
be the administrative hassle one might think. While
unforeseen costs did emerge at Stanford, burdening the
Instructional Television Network, it was, after all, part
of the project's goal to uncover such expenses. On the
other hand, the full potential of resource sharing was
not tapped in this project. Further experimentation must
focus on the interaction capabilities of this medium
within an educational setting, evaluating obtainable
results in light of other mechanisms offering similar
"results." Hence, curriculum-sharing via satellite must
still be phrased in terms of potential. (Strover, 1978)

Another recent experiment in graduate engineering education using
the Communications Technology Satellite involved North Carolina A&T;
Jackson State University, Mississippi; Stanford University; Bell
Northern Research of Canada; and the Rockwell International Science
Center. In this two-day activity, graduate students and faculty
members of two institutions with large minority enrollments had the
opportunity to present and receive technical reports on high-level
research projects. Two-way video and audio channels permitted
face-to-face interaction between participants on the east and west
coasts.

The above experiments were really demonstrations of potential
long-term satellite applications. At a "Conference on Educational
Applications of Satellites" sponsored by the National Institute of
Education (NIE), Lawrence P. Grayson, Chief of the Technology
Applications Division of NIE reported that the Institute would commit
itself to a second major program of support for satellite
applications. "The purpose of this program is to identify uses that
can meet existing educational needs, to demonstrate that the costs can
be kept low enough to be afforded by the users, and to assist a number
of organizations through the transition from having shown that
satellites can be useful in meeting the needs of their constituencies
to implementing operational services." (National Institute of
Education, 1977) In this context, representatives of media-based
engineering education programs have been developing a plan for
implementing an operational satellite delivery service.

An Operational Plan

Past and present programs of media-based systems will have a strong
influence on the development of future services provided by
satellites. The engineering profession can look forward to starting
with an already tried and tested educational service that will be
expanded and enhanced through geostationary satellites having broad
coverage. Televised engineering education is currently reaching a

numerically large, but relatively small proportion, of the population
of over one million working engineers. However, the future
satellite-based delivery service will:

- Deliver regular classroom subjects, generally engineering and
  science courses at the graduate level, beyond present regional
  boundaries served by ITFS, ETV, and slowly delivered videotape;
- Deliver more studio produced, packaged courses to larger
  numbers of users on a timely, efficient basis; and
- Deliver novel, special programs such as short courses,
  seminars, speeches, and emergency engineering-related notices
  which are not now being made available for national
  distribution because of the financial constraints imposed by
  relatively small local audiences.

Though a centralized system, the satellite will permit video
broadcasting of classroom instruction from major American universities
to employed engineers at industrial plants and research laboratories
thoughout the country. It also will permit curriculum sharing and
curriculum enrichment by providing smaller or developing institutions
with access to major university programs. It is anticipated that many
such institutions will want to supplement their curricula. For
example, the Oregon Graduate Center currently lists videotaped courses
from Stanford and MIT in its descriptive literature.

In addition to the video broadcasting described above, the system
will permit the transmission of examinations, lecture notes, and
homework assignments on a subcarrier that will be demodulated and
reproduced separately at each receiving point, thus producing
hardcopy. With this simple system, up to 15 pages of written or
printed material will be transmitted with each hour of video
broadcasting. By one estimate, there are 200,000 facsimile copiers now
in use, and such rapid growth is anticipated that over 500,000 are
expected to be in use by 1985. This technology will prove important in
the implementation of national and international education programs by
satellite.

A data and document retrieval service also will be provided for
each participating university and industrial subscriber. Initially, a
telephone line data terminal will be used to access computer-based
library services and national data banks. A national data bank of
engineering educational services such as abstracts, catalogs of
courses, and consultant services will be accessible through this
system. Data which have been requested will be returned over the
telephone line, or a document will be sent from a video-transmitting
university at the same time as the classroom broadcast by means of the
facsimile machine and subcarrier channel mentioned above. Other new
satellite-based data transmission systems will be explored as they
become available.

Two-way teleconferencing also will be possible with a satellite
system. Two satellite channels will be required whenever face-to-face
conferencing is needed. It is anticipated that teleconferencing will
lead to more effective coordination of many projects and programs among
universities. Indeed, some believe that only in this way can the full

benefits of a national educational consortium, such as AMCEE, be
realized. Currently, key university administrators travel to
occasional meetings then return to their home institutions to relay
plans, but the satellite system will enable working groups of dispersed
faculty and industrialists within a single discipline to undertake
planning and evaluation sessions on a continuing basis.
Teleconferencing also will allow people at widely separated locations
to interact in technical seminars.

Programs will range from standard 30- to 40-hour graduate level
engineering and science courses to short classes of five to ten hours
duration. Transmission of live courses will take place during the
six-hour period when east and west coast universities are in session
(11 a.m. - 5 p.m. Eastern Time; 8 a.m. - 2 p.m. Pacific Time). During
the other available hours, prerecorded materials will be transmitted
for off-the-air recording and use at a convenient time.

Anticipated Satellite Configurations

There are two fundamental system models under consideration: 1) the
independent system in which the satellite transponder connects program
originator and users directly, using only originator-user owned uplinks
and downlinks as shown in Figure 5; and 2) the dependent system in
which part of the system belongs to another agency such as the National
Public Radio (NPR) of the Public Broadcasting Service (PBS) as shown in
Figure 6.

With the independent system, one university will send a signal
through a satellite directly to other universities and participating
company sites. A receiving university might then retransmit the signal
over its local system. The dependent system will be tied to PBS earth
stations (both radio and television) located on or near university
campuses. Programming will be sent and received through shared
terminals, with university-owned control centers handling the
preliminary origination and the subsequent distribution of the sent and
received signals.

A combined system in which shared and independently-owned terminals
are used is technically possible also. The choice of independent,
dependent, or mixed systems will depend on the availability and costs
of the satellites and related components. Currently, a major
political-corporate struggle is underway to determine the appropriate
uses of available frequencies; the outcome of this will have a
significant impact on the direction of all future satellite services in
the United States. Therefore, engineering educators are in a "wait and
see" mode in their planning at the present time.

Economic Factors

The media-based university engineering programs generally consider
only the capital costs and day-to-day operating costs of their
broadcast or videotape systems. Faculty salaries are covered by the
university budgets and are not included in the media-based system

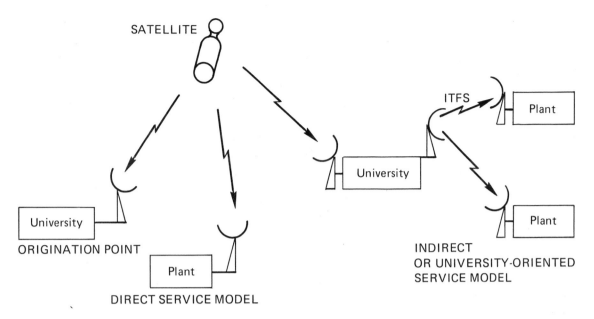

FIGURE 5 Independent system model.

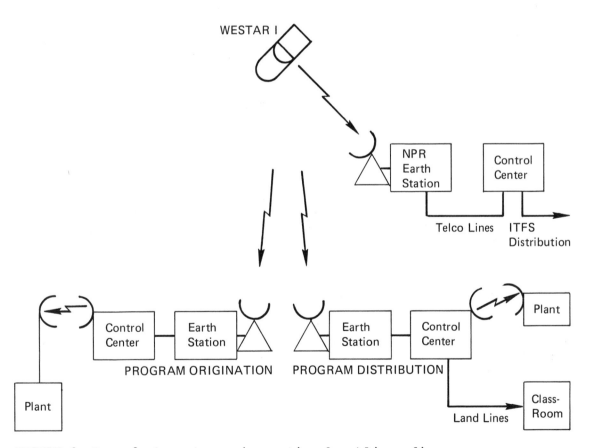

FIGURE 6 Dependent system using national public radio.

costs. Adding a satellite delivery mode on top of the current systems requires careful cost analysis, as the hourly transponder fee can range from $100 to $1,000. The earth terminal equipment cost also must be taken into consideration.

If one assumes a satellite rental fee of $300 per hour, a course fee of $50 per hour, and that 20 percent of the course fee ($10 per hour) would be set aside to cover the satellite cost, then a minimum of 30 subscribers is needed just to cover the satellite rental cost. It is clear that large aggregated audiences are essential for the system to be economically viable.

An issue currently receiving attention is the role of the federal government in fostering the development and utilization of communications satellites in public service areas, including education. The Committee on Satellite Communications of the Space Application Board of the National Research Council (NRC) recently published a report on this subject. The Committee did not recommend that the federal government, i.e., NASA, provide and operate a public service satellite communications system. However, it strongly supported the option in which "NASA and appropriate user agencies would jointly define, develop, and test (including flight demonstrations) new public service satellite communications systems. In addition, NASA and the user would be jointly responsible for transferring the new system to the appropriate operating agencies." (Committee on Satellite Communications of the Space Applications Board, NRC, 1977)

At this point, it seems that the community of engineering educators developing the plan for an operational satellite delivery service can foresee a break-even or profitable operation in a relatively short amount of time (assuming that marketing projections are valid and counting only hourly satellite rental fees). However, the initial capital required for such a system will be approximately $2 million.

Experience is the primary difference between the operators of media-based systems for delivering engineering education and other public service groups who are seeking federal support for the development of satellite-based systems. Most of the managers of the in-place engineering education systems have operating experience of five to ten years behind them; they are seasoned veterans. They are familiar with the problems of putting course schedules together, distributing them, and enrolling students. They know the costs of high quality media-based instruction, and they know that they depend on income from satisfied users for survival. They have experience in dealing with university administrators and faculty, industrial training directors, engineering managers, and engineering students of varying ages and abilities. This is the single most compelling argument in favor of immediate federal support for the development of a nationwide satellite service for engineering education. Diffusion of the technology to other areas of higher education then can proceed.

Video/Computer Combinations

Despite the rapid decline in the cost of hardware for computing, expenditures in this area by institutions of higher education have not declined. Nevertheless, in computing, the past will probably not be a good guide to the immediate future because the affordable alternatives are multiplying rapidly.

Advances in semiconductor technology have caused incredible changes in the last decade (Flanagan, 1977). Whitney (1977) put these advances in economic perspective as shown in Figure 7, noting that "it takes about 2,000 gates to make a four-function calculator, about 8,000 to make a 16-bit minicomputer, and about 40,000 to make a medium-scale 32-bit computer." His conclusion is generally regarded as true:

> The point of all this is that semiconductor technology is advancing at such a rate that, even before 1980, the cost of processor electronics will not be important. There will be new rules by which to play the computer design game. We must think creatively about what to do with "zero cost" logic. (Whitney, 1977)

In early 1975, computer kits were marketed for about $340 in what might be called the first wave of personal computers. Over 400,000 microcomputers have been sold since then. "Dozens of companies have entered the marketplace with new computers, terminals, disc drives, speech synthesizers, D/A and A/D converters, audio-cassette-recorder interfaces, graphics systems, and other related devices." (Braun, 1977) Today, several computers are being retailed for approximately $900, assembled. These are complete microcomputers with a large-capacity memory, a video monitor, a keyboard, and an audio cassette recorder, all with interfaces, plus the usual processor and power supply. These second generation personal computers feature BASIC, but other computer languages such as FORTRAN IV, APL, and PACAL are readily available. They were on the market two years after the first generation. A wide array of compatible peripheral hardware are available which plug into the unit. For example, a popular color graphic device consists of a single board costing $350 with a definition of 128 x 128 (horizontal x vertical) picture elements which permits the choice of eight colors on a TV monitor in two intensities (Dwyer and Sweer, 1976). Personal computer manufacturers were the star electronics performers of 1979; the three major competitors each more than doubled their output.

Hardware is just part of the revolution. Other evidence includes:

- Publications aimed at the computer amateur and educator: Byte, Dr. Dobb's Journal, Kiloband, Personal Computing, ROM, Creative Computing, People's Computer Company;
- Computer retail stores;
- Computer clubs; and
- Personal computer shows such as the first one in Atlantic City in August, 1976, which drew 5,000 attendees.

Table top machines with the power of an IBM 1620 now retail for under $2,000. By mid-1980, an IBM executive has promised one-third the power of an IBM 370/168 "under a keyboard."

54

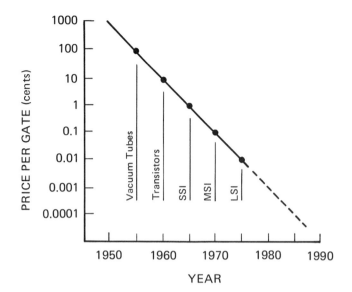

FIGURE 7 Costs of logic gates.

Concurrently with the microprocessor innovations outlined above, progress is being made on videodisc systems targeted for the consumer marketplace. These laser-powered recording systems employ digital signal storage and retrieval which provides data or image storage density that far exceeds that of magnetic recording. "Playback only" optical disk storage systems are available now which offer an economic savings of at least 20 percent compared to other mass frame storage media, e.g., microfilm, microfiche, and film strips. Furthermore, the same disk can store computer codes for interactive electronics and other functions. The principal problem with these first systems is the "read only" memory feature that not only precludes easy editing when used in an interactive CAI authoring mode, but also makes reproduction runs of 100 or more copies necessary if the "playback only" disks are to be competitive in cost with video cassettes for film storage (Schneider, 1977). These shortcomings are recognized, and development work is underway in a number of laboratories to produce laser-powered recording systems with instant playback as a medium for high-speed, mass data storage (Bartolini, et al., 1978).

The promise of inexpensive, rapidly accessible, massive videofiles coupled with the rapidly developing microcomputer technology is stimulating renewed interest in the use of these technologies for educational purposes. An essential new ingredient is the orientation of the device manufacturers toward direct consumer purchase.

Current Status

Many university presidents may welcome the consumer takeover of computing. As shown in Figure 8, the central university computing facilities in the United States spent over $991 million during 1976-77, up from $472 million in 1969-70 (Hamblen, 1977, 1978). Figure 8 distributes these amounts by major computer functions, i.e., instruction, research, and administration. Note the huge increase in dollars over a three-year period. Also note that administrative expenditures grew appreciably faster than instruction and research expenditures. Eighty-two percent of the computer costs for the 1977 fiscal year were paid through the funds of the individual institutions, 7 percent was paid by the federal government agencies and 11 percent by other sources.

The fourth inventory of computers in higher education sponsored by the National Science Foundation (NSF) has just been completed. Table 5 shows the types of instructional use of computers that were reported (Hamblen, 1980).

TABLE 5

USES OF COMPUTING IN ENGINEERING EDUCATION

No. of Institutions Reporting	Type of Use
238	Problem solving
136	Simulation
29	Computer-assisted testing
43	Computer-assisted instruction
10	Computer-managed instruction

Source: Hamblen, 1980

Table 6 shows that the cost of computing services for engineering students in courses which required a computer rose from $45 per student in a course in 1969 to $71 per student in a course in 1976. Note that engineering is now the most expensive discipline per student in a course, but lags behind computer science and business in total resources demanded.

Although not shown in Table 6, Hamblen reports a slight drop in the number of courses (12 percent) and engineering students (22 percent) in 1976 as compared to 1969. On the other hand, the total resources consumed climbed from $10.9 million in 1969 to $13.3 million in 1976. Both trends are puzzling since computing costs are clearly decreasing and total engineering enrollments have risen sharply during the interval. It should be noted, however, that the survey response rate also dropped from 75 percent in 1969-70 to 58 percent in 1976-77, and no attempt was made to extrapolate the data. Indeed, an interpretative analysis of these data on computing in instruction is not yet available; inquiries may be directed to Carl Zinn, University of Michigan.

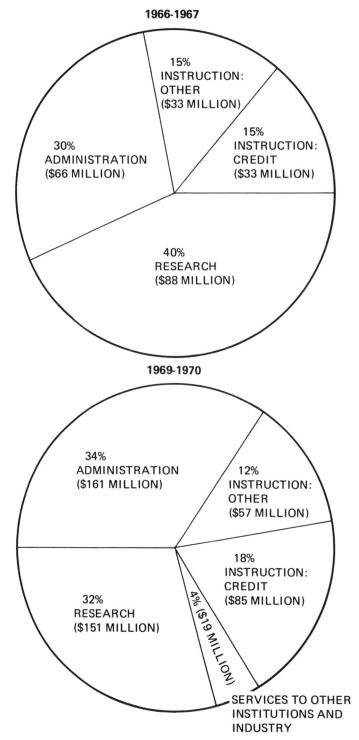

SOURCE: Hamblen, 1977.

FIGURE 8   Estimated Distribution of Expenditures for Instruction Research and Administrative Uses of Computers in U.S. Higher Education 1966–67 and 1969–70.

TABLE 6

COST PER STUDENT PER COURSE FOR VARIOUS
DISCIPLINE AREAS, 1969-70 and 1976-77

Discipline Area	Number of Courses 1976-77	Number of Students 1976-77	Value of Computer Use (in Millions) 1976-77	Cost per Student per Course 1969-70	Cost per Student per Course 1976-77
Computer Science	8651	292,921	$17.2	$78	$59
Engineering	7356	187,877	13.3	45	71
Business	5320	259,003	14.8	44	57
Math/statistics	3716	125,145	4.8	42	38
Physical Sciences	2418	84,053	3.1	45	37
Social Sciences	3090	85,621	2.3	36	26
Education	1088	31,292	.7	27	24
Environmental and Life Science	2408	69,825	1.8	--	26
All Other	3962	133,175	5.1	54	38

The above table shows the numbers of courses that involved computer usage during 1976-77, the numbers of students enrolled in those courses, and the value of the computer services by discipline area. These figures are based upon report summaries and are not extrapolated estimates; the 1969-70 survey had a 75% response rate and the 1976-77 survey only a 58% response.

Source: Hamblen, 1980.

The cost of hardware amortization during the 1976-77 academic year is 40 percent of the cost of computer services cited above. The personnel support services for the computing facilities, maintenance contracts, expendable supplies, and software purchases generally take the other 60 percent. These costs of ownership also will shift to the individual, or perhaps in the initial stages of transition, to the academic departments in which the new computers will reside.

The early stage of this shift of ownership is already evident on many campuses. Some major university research users of computers are now purchasing very advanced minicomputers to perform rather large simulation calculations, as well as for special-purpose data reduction (e.g., Lykos, 1977). Some of these machines are linked to the central computing facility by telephone or cable. It is reasonable to expect that the new personal computers, which will be capable of performing many of the instructional computation tasks assigned to students, also will be interconnected with central computing facilities when the need arises (Zinn, 1980). Organizational problems centering around funding patterns and operational control will probably increase temporarily as the process described above spreads and evolves. However, just as the introduction of paperback books shifted ownership of some supplemental readings into the hands of students without closing the university libraries, central university computing facilities can be expected to thrive on administrative and interactive services. Some large data bases and simulations used in instruction also will reside in such centers. However, the trend is clearly toward decentralized computing for instruction.

Some of the major instructional applications of computers with particular emphasis on computer graphics and the potential of the videodisc should be highlighted. These will be discussed as useful variations on the three instructional goals of ET mentioned earlier: 1) to lower costs; 2) to individualize instruction; and 3) to provide unique experiences (Hooper, 1974).

Computers to Lower Costs

Today, few people seriously consider lowering costs an argument for computing in instruction. The early literature abounds with cost-effectiveness discussions, but any honest comparison of computerized teaching costs with conventional teaching costs per hour are disappointing, perhaps by a factor of three in the recent past. University-based advocates generally employ "anyhow" accounting--"we are going to do it anyhow"--when discussing costs. Perhaps the most honest cost quote of the day is that from Control Data Corporation for its Programmed Logic for Automatic Teaching Operations (PLATO) service; it is fogged only by a disregarding of the early federal investment of over $15 million for system development. A monthly lease of a single PLATO terminal with all interconnections and curricula-use charges is about $1,000. If used at a normal rate of 125 hours per month, the resulting cost is approximately $8.00 per student-contact-hour. Using effectiveness as an argument is only partially successful, since the

results have been mixed in the larger computer instruction projects as
will be discussed later. However, few educators doubt that there are
gains to be made in this area. Hooper (1974) notes that assessing
"cost-effectiveness is, after all, only a means to an end" and
"cost-effectiveness arguments generally, are a mine field of good (and
bad) intentions."

The latter point focuses on a major failing of government
procedures with regard to computers in education to date. No sustained
effort to enlarge the numbers of educators working on computer
applications has been undertaken recently. Less then 5 percent of the
nation's engineering colleges now receive external support to explore
these issues on a broad scale over time. Rather, until recently, two
large projects (PLATO and TICCIT) have commanded virtually all federal
support for almost a decade. Now, these programs also have been forced
into the marketplace. The initial selling rhetoric for these
large-scale projects was "cost effectiveness." If we have learned from
this recent experience, we will not force educators who seek to apply
computers to instruction to make premature cost savings claims again.

At the local level, universities treat computing as an add-on cost
to traditional instruction. The issues are: 1) what can be afforded;
and 2) how to get the best utilization of the central facility. The
value of computing in instruction is generally conceded without much
study. All major institutions support major computing facilities.

Computers to Individualize Instruction

Active learners _interacting_ with a computer-based tutor that can
diagnose and test, as well as quickly present a variety of sequences of
instruction, is the goal of computer-aided instruction (CAI) and, to a
lesser extent, computer-managed instruction (CMI). The approach builds
on the research on the early programmed learning machines but adds the
flexibility of massive computer record keeping of individual
performance. Thus, CAI also promises interactive course authoring
based on student performance data. Merrill (1971) discusses the
components of a cybernetic instructional system in a general manner.

Sugarman (1978) reviews the state of the art in practice with
illustrative examples.

> The lure of computer-aided instruction (CAI) is once again
> being felt by those who have maintained their interest in this
> problem-ridden educational tool and believe that advances in
> the technology will give it another chance. In the late
> 1960's, it was supposedly going to revolutionize the learning
> process; the best teachers were going to write "courseware"
> (interactive education computer programs) that would be
> nationally distributed. Students would learn rapidly and
> efficiently. However, reality turned out to be quite different
> from the dream - so far.

A few people did take the time to study the medium's potential and did produce outstanding computer educational material. But, CAI development, which has remained in the hands of a relatively small community of experts, has yet to develop as much courseware as had been predicted. Except for grade-school drill and practice, it also has yet to overcome the general reluctance of the educational community to adopt it on a wide scale. (Sugarman, 1978)

Appendix D reproduces Sugarman's article, "A Second Chance for Computer-Aided Instruction: What Networking Promised But Didn't Deliver May be Developed at the Local Level as Hardware Costs Drop." It provides a good summary of the status of CAI today.

A 1967 review (Bushnell and Allen) cited 26 CAI/CMI projects underway at the time. Sugarman's 1978 review cites only nine programs. Perhaps the most refreshing change promised by inexpensive, widely distributed hardware is the opportunity to expand greatly the number of educators involved in CAI and CMI. The educational benefits of such an expansion would not be limited to a more rapid dispersion of CAI in institutions; it also would provide many educators with experience in one of the most demanding ET tasks, the creation of CAI courseware. Interactive authoring of CAI materials based on detailed student performance and attitude surveys maintained by the computer cannot be simulated in other media. Furthermore, the computer format requires explicit organization which can be audited and transferred. In principle, the PLATO program allowed this authoring experience to be dispersed, but cost and other constraints have prevented wide-scale exposure. The federal government should undertake a sustained program of funding which would allow educators, particularly those in the engineering and physical science areas, to experiment with the production of CAI courseware. Such a program should support the operating expenses associated with the necessary research, as well as prototype equipment purchases. At an annual funding level of $90 million, a well-managed program could stimulate many fruitful joint ventures between educators and equipment manufacturers.

From Table 1 of Appendix D, note that work is now underway to develop a stand-alone PLATO V terminal. Similarly, Heuston (1977) reports on work underway by TICCIT developers to produce a demonstration of biology instruction on a new videodisc player coupled to a microprocessor and keyboard. Perhaps, the conversion of the existing courseware to new, stand-alone machines is logically a first step. The evaluation results are not persuasive however (e.g., Alderman, et al., 1978, with responses), though students clearly "like" the computerized instruction (e.g., Magidson, 1978).

Results from a program employing randomly accessed video frames from a disc and ITV from a tape were reported by Hayman and Lord (1972). This computer-managed instruction (CMI) system used a computer-based management strategy formulated from the taxonomy of Bloom (1956); a mini-computer interface to mass storage (CDC 6400); a rotating video memory disc to provide 450 video images on the top surface and a flying head to search for the required image, and to

transfer the signal to the underside of the disc where a fixed
buffer-head transferred the signal to a TV monitor at the student
station. Brief videotaped presentations were stored on a videotape
player modified to allow random access and remote control. Although it
was constrained by yesterday's hardware, this development work also is
a point of departure for other engineering educators who seek to
combine video and computing for individualized instruction today.

The real promise of the videodisc coupled with a microcomputer is
decentralization. If the hardware costs do not dominate, then
computer-based courseware production can be widely explored. Recall
that ITV hardware costs represent only a small fraction of the total
cost of video-based instruction. Therefore, inexpensive, local
courseware development flourishes. Yet, very elaborate ITV productions
by the BBC for the Open University also can be justified; these cost
10,000 times more than a candid classroom production. Now that
hardware costs do not demand centralization, policy-makers should
encourage wide exploration of computer courseware development
procedures. The pool of educators seriously interested in the
application of computers to instruction would be enlarged most
effectively by this strategy.

In late 1975, the NSF sponsored a workshop entitled "Ten Year
Forecast for Computers and Communications: Implications for Education
- 1985." The resulting publication (Seidel and Rubin, 1977) has
thoughtful articles on the impact of large-scale, integrated circuits
and storage technology on educational computing systems, as well as the
impact of improved interfaces with the learner. S. Papert (1977) gives
a seductive argument on learning environments for children, and he
concludes:

> Surely I have said enough to make the point that
> formulating the task as design for education in a
> technologically rich future leads very quickly into areas
> of research which are totally neglected, indeed quite
> unsuspected, by the community of professionals in
> 'education research and innovation.' There must in the
> world be tens of thousands of people struggling to
> understand what happens in a classroom where children are
> asked to do sums with pencil on square paper. Some of
> them try to improve matters by having the children do the
> same sums on computer terminals. I do not think it is my
> business to criticize or judge the value of all this. But
> I cannot help being overwhelmed by the fact that there
> must be ten thousand or more people doing that for each
> one person who has the other kind of design process of
> which I have tried to give you a glimpse. And I suggest
> that what happens in ten years depends very sensitively on
> whether our society decides that it can afford a small
> shift in this ratio. So perhaps the problem is more
> political than technological. And if the political aspect
> depends on how well we can convey an alternate vision,
> then perhaps it is even more poetical than political.
> (Papert, 1977)

It is worth noting that the British apparently have decided on CMI as the most promising route. In CMI, of course, the computer may be on the periphery of the learning process; rather, the computer is employed as a manager. Records are kept and tests are given, scored, and analyzed. Students are routed through course modules on the basis of learning ability.

> Computer based learning is now entrenched in the UK; the question is no longer whether it will happen but how it will evolve. The major factor is cost. Software and hardware are expensive. Computer assisted learning and computer managed learning are add-on costs, like audio-visual aids and educational television. Notwithstanding, the government is betting on them. The Council for Educational Technology has been given a four-year follow-on grant from the government to disseminate and coordinate computer assisted learning and computer managed learning, so clearly there is interest in maintaining the momentum. (Adams, 1978)

Some of the old distinctions between CAI and CMI are fading. For example, a national conference on CMI held in Chicago in November, 1974, spent considerable time debating the distinctions (Mitzel, 1974), and the first PLATO Courseware Catalog (CDC, 1978) contains courses employing PLATO, videotapes, and printed texts.

A review of the research results from CMI was given by Hawkridge (1974). An excellent example of CMI in medical education is reported by R. E. Pengov in the proceedings cited above (Mitzel, Part II, 1974). Pengov describes the Ohio State University College of Medicine CMI system, which is used as a supplemental instructional tool on campus, as a continuing education delivery system for 15 other locations, and as an alternate path through some basic science courses for medical students. In the latter mode, CMI is popular with students for the time savings it allows through self-pacing.

Word processing offers another example of computers to individualize instruction. In the last few years, the offices of many engineering groups in industry and government have added equipment and supporting software to assist in the preparation of reports, specifications, and many other documents. University faculty engaged in research are increasingly employing similar equipment, and in the near future they will surely be attracted to the application of word processing to assist student engineers in the preparation of assignments. The automatic recognition of misspelled words alone will relieve the instructor of a time consuming task. Many other features of word processing are sure to be exploited by faculty who have this equipment to assist them in their work.

Computers to Provide Unique Experiences

Engineering education abounds with examples in which computing
does, indeed, provide unique experiences. Hooper attempts to catalog
these as follows:

- Get first-hand experience of more realistic problems and
  experiments, without the student getting bogged down in
  mathematics and data analysis;
- Explore and practice numerical approaches to problem solving,
  thus complementing traditional analytical procedures, and,
  given these numerical techniques, the student can then tackle
  the more realistic problems;
- To integrate different approaches and disciplines in an
  authentic, multivariate, simulation model;
- To develop skills of synthesizing as well as analyzing (circuit
  design may be best learnt by designing circuits rather than
  analyzing circuits already designed);
- To close the gap between theory and practice, lecture and lab
  session, by being able to manipulate in practice theoretical
  concepts, changing, for example, the input values and
  parameters of a given model to test a given hypothesis;
- To develop problem-solving skills particularly with regard to
  decision-making, for example in the planning of scientific
  experiments or in the carrying out of a medical diagnosis; [and]
- To perform simulated experiments which are expensive,
  dangerous, time-consuming, impossible to do in the normal
  science teaching laboratory. (Hooper, 1974)

Clearly the above partial listing of unique educational experiences
made possible by computing illustrates the almost endless variety of
instructional goals which could be catalogued. In the opinion of the
authors, these educational uses of computers are both the most fruitful
and, from the point of view of external support, the most neglected
applications of computing. The examples provided in the following
subsections are illustrative only and are given in the hope that they
will convey some of the excitement which knowledgeable experts share
for the role of computing in providing unique learning experiences.

Problem Solving, Simulation, Laboratories: If personal, or at
least much less costly, computing systems become widely dispersed in
engineering colleges, the faculty who would direct the use of these
facilities to improve instruction could profit from the following
insight.

> For the undergraduate curriculum in mathematics, physics, and
> engineering, and most other sciences, the maximum return on a
> modest investment of developmental effort comes from work in
> problem-solving, simulation, and laboratory data analysis, in
> that order. Furthermore, I contend that work in these
> computational uses leads to a qualitative improvement in the

teaching of the essential subject matter of these courses, in
that it makes some central concepts possible to teach that were
not possible or very difficult before. Third, I contend that
these three categories of use develop in the student a sense of
mastery of a powerful general tool. And, finally, I contend
that these uses, which are student-dominated rather than
computer-dominated, are more in keeping with the liberal
tradition of inquiry. (Luehrmann, 1971)

Outside of science and engineering education, one might sustain an
argument that computers must be programmed by teachers to become a part
of the educational process. However, the very practice of engineering
is being changed dramatically by computers, so student proficiency in
computing per se is a universal goal.

Affordable, stand-alone hardware has the potential of improving the
transferability of courseware from institution to institution. The
cost of courseware development will progressively become the dominant
cost of computing, because hardware costs are rapidly declining while
labor-intensive courseware is becoming more expensive. Perhaps the day
will come when, in order to transfer an attractive instructional
program, an educator will simply purchase the specific machine employed
by the developer and negotiate a lease or purchase of the desired
courseware. This approach would assure transferability. Of course,
this approach is essentially the inverse of all efforts to date, such
as CONDUIT (1977).

To guide educators through this transition, federal officials
should design a number of new programs aimed at encouraging the
transfer of courseware. These diverse efforts might include
sponsorship of the following: consumers' unions to evaluate courseware
which is operational on specific machines in specified disciplines, and
to publish findings (Braun, 1977); lectureships to enhance personal
knowledge transfer among educators in a discipline who are in different
institutions; workshops and summer institutes for faculty at leading
regional institutions; and media-based, short, packaged courses for
educators to use for in-service training, with laboratory experiences
designed around popular stand-alone equipment.

The initial impact of the personal computers may be centered in
high schools. The efforts of Truxal and Braun, SUNY-Stony Brook, to
influence minority students in grades 9 though 12 was mentioned
earlier. They have found that simply making a personal calculator
available on loan to minority students in Chicago high schools (with no
formal instruction) stimulated a very significant improvement in
mathematics performance (Diehl, 1978). Others have reported similar
findings (Suydam, 1978). More recently, Truxal and Braun have been
experimenting with PET 2001 microcomputers in three Chicago high
schools, and, in one instance, the machine is transported from the
school to a neighborhood youth center after-hours and on weekends.

In the simulation mode, the computer becomes a device to simulate
physical reality in the form of governing equations, laboratory
experiments, or probabilistic processes. Thus, simulation applications
of the computer can be as varied as the historical role of

experimentation has been in the education of engineers. The computer is, of course, not a substitute for some real laboratory experiences. Instead, the simulations are most effective when coupled with traditional experiments to provide experience with a wider range of variables or to illustrate theories about microscopic behaviors that are not directly observable. An outstanding example of the power of computing in improving microscopic insights was published by Rahman and Stillinger (1971). This pioneering effort to simulate liquid water at the molecular level has stimulated many more investigations on the modeling of matter (e.g., Lykos, 1978b). In this same vein, Deardorf (1970) simulated three-dimensional turbulent channel flow using the basic time-varying equations of motion to provide a detailed insight into this complicated phenomenon, an insight that was not available before the advent of today's computing power. Computer-generated movies or videotapes may be used to summarize this research work for students (Science, 1978). And, in the future, expanded capacities in local computers may enable classes to interact with these models in a laboratory manner as well (Wilson, 1975).

The gap between industrial practice and the university laboratory is widening rapidly. The emergence of powerful new measuring instruments and control devices is outpacing the equipment budgets of universities. Each of the new industrial instruments has a microprocessor and digital memory as an integral part of the device. Many of the instruments have built-in data analysis programs which alter the traditional lab procedures fundamentally. These same instruments are being employed by engineers in practice to assist in the automation of industrial processes and machinery (Oliver, 1977). Indeed, young graduates with skills in the applications of these "intelligent" instruments are in greatest demand today. Yet, unless more effective funding mechanisms are developed, the engineering colleges will become progressively more poorly equipped to offer instruction with modern instrumentation. This hardware problem should be addressed by industries concerned with the manufacturing and application of the new generation of instruments. Perhaps the National Research Council could study the issue and make recommendations for needed actions, such as new government incentives to bring university instruction in this area up to acceptable standards.

Combined Media for Case Studies: Bell and Brenchley (1972) use the case study approach to involve students in community environmental problems. They created a data base for a reference community to defuse local political implications and to minimize time lost searching for data. The case contains 200 pages of descriptive information on such topics as government, public works, health and welfare, socio-economic conditions, climate, commerce and industry, and recreation. The file also contains 25 figures and 46 tables. Historical data trends are given, and city and county environmental health ordinances are included. This rather massive file is used as the basis for several computer simulation games:

- Air pollution - "Air Quality Display Model," (Environmental Protection Agency, Washington, D.C., 1969, there are later versions of APEX as well);
- Water quality - "Simulation of Water Quality in Streams and Canals - DOSAG-1," (Pub. 202-974, Texas Water Development Board, September 1970);
- Solid waste management - "DISCUSS - A Solid Waste Management Game," (A.J. Klee, IEEE Transactions, Vol. GE-8, No. 3, July 1970).

The integration of these activities into a common, transportable format requires massive data and program storage. The entire effort might be given additional motivational impact by selective use of ITV. Instructional programs such as this are good candidates for videodisc systems.

Interactive Graphics: Computer-aided design (CAD) is a unique experience that is hard to simulate without interactive graphics. Most computers today are operated in a batch-job environment for economic reasons. This may maximize machine utilization, but it can result in very inefficient use of human intellectual power. Braun (1977) likens it to "blowing into a clarinet or plucking a banjo string and waiting till tomorrow [be fair: a half hour!] to hear the note you played!" When interactive computing is aided by graphic displays, the learner or designer has a powerful tool (Bork, 1974). The research literature is not convincing in this matter, but few educators doubt the effectiveness of graphic presentations. The major deterrent to utilization to date has been the relatively high cost of hardware for computer graphics. Appendix D gives some illustrations of current use. With few exceptions, most use of computer graphics on campus has been in conjunction with research projects due to the expense involved.

Bork (1977) outlines the technical requirements for an effective graphic system for instruction, and, looking at the potential of the videodisc at the 1975 conference cited previously, he states:

> Although the developers of videodisc systems have thought primarily of using the videodisc for bringing movies into the home, such videodiscs, used in stand-alone systems, could have a combination of video sequences, audio sequences, slides, and computer code, all on the same inexpensive disc. Thus, a videodisc might hold a complete elaborate teaching dialog that the student employs at a stand-alone display, complete with slides, video sequences, and the necessary computer code. Or, it might contain the code for a full language, such as APL, along with a full set of materials, including video and slides, for learning that language. Thus, the videodisc would allow a full multimedia approach, combining the computer with other media.

Finally, I want to state strongly my belief that meetings
such as the current one are absolutely essential.
Educational computer use is still, I believe, in a very
early stage. We must look very carefully into the
future, seeing the technological possibilities and trying
to mold developments in directions conducive to use in
learning environments. Often, pedagogical uses of
technological devices have followed the technology; for
effective educational use, this is the wrong order. It
is important to examine desirable futures from the
standpoint of improving learning environments and to
influence the development of the technology to create
these environments. I am particularly suspicious of
arguments from technology, arguments which go along the
lines of 'I have a very powerful piece of hardware,' or
'I have a very powerful software idea.' The sensible
approach is to start from actual learning and teaching
problems; these then should influence the hardware,
languages, and computer techniques. (Bork, 1977)

Rensselaer Polytechnic Institute (RPI) has made a major investment
in interactive computer graphics in engineering education. Wozny
(1978) argues that:

The real key to computer graphics is giving students
enough time on the machine. The computer is nothing more
than a dynamic extension of their textbook. Just as
students generally require several readings before fully
understanding a concept, they should be accorded similar
access privileges to a computer. An effective facility
must be large enough to handle such a demand.

Computer graphics is effective in engineering education
because it emphasizes intuition rather than exact
calculations. For years, engineering students used
computers simply to get answers expressed to 10 decimal
places. In order to understand the underlying
relationships, the student generally had to print a number
of solutions during one computer run and then try to
interpret the tables of numbers or the crude plots from
the line printer. Computer graphics overcomes both of
these shortcomings because: (1) an interactive system
must provide fast turnaround by definition; and (2) its
drawing and plotting capability is of high quality. Thus,
graphics gives a student immediate reinforcement in a
natural conversational graphic mode. Refresh graphics
adds the capability of animation. The pedagogical
significance of changing with a light pen the location of
a single charged particle in an electric field with other
charged particles, and watching all the field lines move
as if they were rubber bands cannot be overstated! The

pedagogical advantages of computer graphics in perspective
are:

- visualization (one picture is worth a...)
- animation (motion)
- interactiveness (what if?)
- intuition (instead of exact calculations)

As stated earlier, the trend in industrial design is
toward increased use of computer graphics. Several
industries have documented large savings when graphics is
used. Graphics offers the design engineer the ability to
interact, evaluate, and modify designs directly in the
graphics mode. In certain areas where the product is well
understood, designs bypass the experimental verification
stage entirely and go directly into production! In
effect, the computer solution via graphics becomes a
pseudo-experimental verification.

Industrial advantages for using graphics are:
- eliminates expensive experimentation
- reduces time between design and production
- provides required human intervention in complex
  designs
- reduces engineering design time thru
  human/computer optimization. (Wozny, 1978)

The article cited above also describes the use of imported software
in electronic circuit analysis, finite element structural analysis,
digital filter design, integrated mechanisms, and multivariable systems
design. The use rather than the coding of these complex programs is
stressed. Some engineering educators place so much emphasis on
analysis and coding that students often are deprived of the opportunity
to use a completed package in a design mode. The RPI facility also
supports development work on new programs.

The need to develop facilities with similar purposes at each
engineering college is a pressing issue in engineering education
today. The creation of a national interest group or association,
perhaps within the American Society for Engineering Education (ASEE),
would be a beginning step. However, at least a dozen prototype
facilities should be funded throughout the nation in the next one to
three years to serve as organizational and operational models, as
clearinghouses for vendors and educators, and as centers for the
creation of outreach materials aimed at informing educators within a
given discipline or region. The task is too large and important not to
design a dispersed support system for both educators and administators
to encourage the rapid, meaningful development of interactive graphics
and computing in engineering education.

Goals for Computing

Unfortunately, the introduction of computing is highly fragmented in most colleges, and a student's experience depends largely on the particular instructors contacted. The engineering student's exposure to subject matter is highly structured; the curricula is the product of much local faculty discussion and is carefully reviewed by external accreditors. But, the role of computing rarely receives this attention, despite its impact on student learning. Computing is not neglected today, just rarely coordinated.

Faculty profitably could spend more time discussing the curricula. To stimulate a fresh look, Lykos (1975) encouraged faculty of the Illinois Institute of Technology to use M. F. Rubinstein's book, Patterns of Problem Solving (Prentice-Hall, 1975), as a point of departure. Roles for computing then could be put into the general framework of problem solving. The participating faculty engaged in a computer-based laboratory which used a modern simulation language, GASP-IV (Pritsker, 1974), to accommodate the modeling of discrete state, continuous state, and hybrid systems.

Some examples of instructional computing today may be found in these references: Blum, et al., 1971; CONDUIT, 1977; and Zinn, 1980. The U.S. Naval Academy also should be cited as an institution which has made an intensive effort to employ the computer for instruction. Adams and Rogers (1975) review the efforts made in Annapolis in engineering education. Some recent work on computer-augmented video systems for instruction at the Naval Academy was published by Pollack (1978) and Prestia (1978).

Research Applications

No attempt will be made to cite the countless applications which computing has today in engineering research at universities. It is a rare graduate student who does not employ the computer in some fashion in research. Computer movies, cited earlier, may be an output that could be transferred readily to instruction, and, of course, ideas from research are carried by the professor to the classroom.

University-based researchers probably will face a new set of facility problems in the coming decade. Faculty demands to decentralize instructional computing will divert university funds from the central computing facility. Therefore, few universities will have the funds necessary to upgrade the central facility so that local computers might keep abreast of the power made possible by inexpensive microelectronics. The local administrative goal is more likely to be the maintenance of existing central computing services at a lower cost in order to permit funding of decentralized instructional facilities. The net effect probably will be to stagnate the "upper end" of the computing power available to many university researchers.

Chemists have recognized the problem outlined above already, and, with the support of the Department of Energy (DOE) and NSF, have created a National Center for Computation in Chemistry at a DOE facility in Berkeley. Approximately $6 million was invested over a three-year period in this facility which is built around a CAC 7600. Background information about the events which led to this federal investment in chemistry research may be found in Bigeleisen, et al. (1975) and Gilbert, et al. (1974). This facility is now in a phasing-down stage and may cease operations in the near future. On the other hand, the National Center for Atmospheric research in Boulder, Colorado, successfully operates a CRAY-1 for university and resident staff. Clearly, engineering research could benefit from a few regional centers as well. Each should operate very large-scale, user-oriented computing facilities, emphasizing a specific engineering discipline. The National Academy of Engineering should undertake a feasibility study to provide specific direction.

Impediments

Many of the past impediments to computing in education are traceable to the relatively high cost of hardware; therefore, most universities want to maximize utilization of a central facility. Denk (1976) reviews current practices at universities under five support categories: technical and systems; materials; personnel; faculty training; and availability, both economic and administrative. The age of "Big Blue," on which Denk reflects, soon will be yielding to decentralization that will bring a new set of issues. At the policy level, some concern is expressed about the lack of government programs and policies regarding computing.

> Due to major investments made several decades ago, the U.S. is the worldwide leader in computer technology. However, due to our laissez-faire approach to the support of technological innovation, other nations are now challenging that position. They are systematically investing large sums of money in computer research and are restructuring their educational systems to emphasize computing so they may exploit the full potential of computers in all segments of their societies.

> Some feel that our current national policy, or the lack of one, will greatly affect our Nation's future level of productivity and our world position in science and technology for many years to come. Many feel that we must undertake an urgent, comprehensive review of our national policy toward technological innovation and with it our policy toward academic research, development, and instruction in the use of computers. (Molnar, 1977)

IV.
HUMAN AND ECONOMIC IMPEDIMENTS

The organizational and environmental impediments to more rapid use of educational technology (ET) must be recognized. Broadly categorized, these impediments are of two kinds: limited human resources and limited economic resources.

Fourth Revolution Delayed: On Campus

Any frontal attack aimed at increasing capital investment in ET and reducing operating costs by replacing teachers is doomed to failure in higher education. Faculty involvement in institutional governance is erratic, a product of a highly decentralized community. Taken as a whole, it would be a rare university that would opt for large-scale adoption of ET. In fact, university budgeting procedures generally preclude the economic trade off, because all capital goods are expensed the year of purchase. The goal of improving education at a reasonable cost, or of improving productivity at the course level (as described by Willey, Appendix B), is not only politically safer to advocate, but also it is the wisest approach to take, given the lack of persuasiveness of ET to date. In our public school systems, upon which taxpayers have a rather direct impact, thousands of teachers did not return to work for the 1978, 1979, and 1980 school years, and at least a half-million students were out of school for awhile in Philadelphia, Boston, Chicago, Cleveland, New Orleans, Seattle, and elsewhere. The disputes between school boards and teachers seemed unusually angry. Rhetoric flourished; solutions did not.

> In the post-Sputnik era, taxpayer contributions to education have doubled, tripled, quadrupled, while test scores of high school graduates suggest we are turning out products with an intellectual capacity somewhere between animal and vegetable. (Buchanan, 1978)

This is not a good environment for innovation, however desirable we consider such a goal.

71

Affordable instructional technology is now being produced for direct purchase by the learner. Hand-held calculators are an excellent example. The value of the device is so apparent that essentially every engineering student owns one. The half-inch videocassette machines, videodiscs, and personal computers are being produced today by manufacturers in an attempt to create a consumer market in addition to an institutional market. Speak and Spell is an exciting new $50 learning aid from TI (Texas Instruments) that teaches children how to spell by pronouncing each word, then interactively grading and scoring the learner. It is built around a voice synthesizer on a single chip, a technology that will spawn a flood of new TI (Texas Instruments) products that can talk (Business Week, 1978).

Commercial mass marketing directly to the learner has not been seriously considered an alternative for ET before. All previous studies have assumed an introduction through institutional budgets and classical curricula (e.g., Tickton, 1970; PSAC, 1967; Carnegie Commission, 1972; and Bugliarello, 1974). The pattern described is circular: the high cost of software; the lack of effective national distribution; and, hence, little development of software.

Special purpose devices with fixed algorithms, like Speak and Spell, are an attractive alternative, if the special purposes that are developed happen to include the items you wish to learn. A device like the read-only videodisc in its present configuration, however, is a good example of how a technology can easily be designed for the marketplace in such a way as to preclude wide-scale development of courseware in higher education. The technology of making a "master" clearly must be modified, if wide-scale development of instructional materials is to proceed. Nevertheless, ten years from now, a review of current ET activities surely will include many more examples because the hardware is becoming much more affordable and a new generation of young instructors will have an impact.

The focus away from hardware, which may come inexpensively in great variety, and toward the instructional goals for ET will surely benefit all. Discipline research is now accepted by engineering faculty as a way of life, a never ending process, because external funding has made wide-scale participation possible. Faculty time, graduate assistants, support staff, as well as specialized, ever-changing hardware are annually allocated in peer-reviewed, national competition. Efficiency is rarely an issue; instead, the quality of the endeavor is judged for its intellectual and, in engineering at least, its practical value. There is great diversity.

The external stimuli for this revolution in campus activity is not a secret; the revolution could not have been wrought by formula funding, by a single agency, or at a small fraction of the cost that has been incurred. While there are key national centers for certain specialized facilities and "think tanks," research policy-makers have generally sought wide participation and have found talent throughout the nation. Professional meetings, publications, and awards support local efforts.

The integration of ET in universities to improve education should,

like discipline research, be process-oriented, not product-oriented;
should be a sustained effort, not the product of occasional Requests
for Proposals; and should involve many more talented people than it
does today in work ranging from immediate local applications to basic
research in artificial intelligence. Compelling demonstrations of
instructional technology will become commonplace once the level of
human effort reaches a certain threshold and the hardware is
distributed widely (Lipson, 1977).

Yet, more external stimuli are essential. Most state universities
are embedded in a bureaucracy which bears a great resemblance to social
service programs. More often than not, innovation is actively
discouraged when there are negative budget incentives for increased
productivity. Private universities are constrained by tight budgets
and, of course, by federal regulations which pervade all of higher
education. Caretaker styles of university administration prosper
today. Therefore, foundations and agencies that want to encourage the
appropriate use of ET should pay careful attention to organizational
situations. Indeed, the use of not-for-profit corporations, perhaps
with close university ties, should be explored.

Rothenberg and Morgan (1975) report on two case studies of
innovation in the educational service sector: "Sesame Street" and the
Children's Television Workshop; and Patrick Suppes' computer-aided
instruction (CAI) work in the Institute of Mathematical Studies in
Social Sciences at Stanford as well as in the Computer Curriculum
Corporation. The studies provide details on the nature of the problem
and the history of the innovation, the subsector or environment, the
initiating unit, the innovation, techniques affecting adoption, the
adopters, the users, and the impact of the innovation. In both of
these successful ET efforts, the need arose for a new organizational
structure.

Engineering Education: Off Campus

Fortunately, most outreach programs are so new that bureaucratic
constraints are far less inhibiting than in other areas of university
endeavor. The cardinal rule is pay-as-you-go, i.e., self-sufficiency.
New enterprises often display considerable entrepreneurial spirit in
carrying out their missions. The client for off-campus extensions of
graduate education and continuing education appears willing to pay for
services delivered. Similarly, foreign programs have well developed
funding sources. The problem areas which require continual subsidy
include programs aimed at junior colleges, at high schools, and at
promoting public understanding of technology.

Resource sharing between colleges in technology-based outreach
programs should be encouraged. Consortia of engineering schools such
as the Association for Media-Based Continuing Education for Engineers
(AMCEE) may prove effective agents of campus change as well as
suppliers of educational services to practicing engineers at their job
sites. Can the faculty resources be effectively pooled through the

AMCEE organization and the use of modern communications technologies? If so, the interaction of engineering faculty with engineers and managers who engage in these graduate and continuing educational programs could provide an operational link between practioners and educators that has long been missing.

V.
SUGGESTIONS FOR IMPROVEMENTS

This concluding section is divided into two parts. The first, Critical Issues, deals with a set of general concerns and institutional issues. To the extent that the three issues identified are judged to be valid, a set of criteria to evaluate specific educational technology (ET) programs and initiatives might be formulated. Clearly, no single set of activities will eliminate the overall problems, but each proposed program could be assessed by the extent to which it trains and rewards faculty, improves the quality and dissemination of materials or resource sharing, and encourages non-bureaucratic responses. The final section summarizes the suggestions for improvement which were integrated into the text.

Critical Issues

James D. Koerner provides a valuable insight into the immediate future of ET. From 1970 to 1976, Koerner served as manager for the Technology in Education program of the Alfred P. Sloan Foundation. During that period, the foundation made about eighty grants totaling approximately $8 million. He is optimistic, noting that:

> Communications technologies are steadily infiltrating the instructional programs of colleges and universities and [experience] suggests that they will do so in the future at an accelerated pace. The question is simply one of how long it will take for technology to become an intimate and integral part of the higher education scene....To speed the development process, certain steps, implicit in the foregoing discussion, need to be taken in higher education. (Koerner, 1977)

75

Training and Rewarding Faculty

Like all other technology, ET requires key human resources for implementation. The appropriate adoption of ET is seriously hindered by a historical lack of a broad-scale, sustained effort to enlarge the number of talented individuals working with media.

> One essential step for the future is for colleges and universities to find ways of multiplying manyfold the number of faculty members experienced in and committed to development work. That is an expensive and time-consuming step, and the difficulty of taking it is suggested by the fact that not a single recognized center now exists anywhere in the country to which interested faculty members from other institutions could be sent for what might be called basic training in educational technology. (Koerner, 1977)

Academic faculty lacking personal exposure to effective applications of ET are often less than enthusiastic about non-traditional instruction methods. To the extent that this is a product of natural conservatism, then engineering faculty react no differently than do other faculty. However, to the extent that issues associated with the design and operation of hardware configurations and systems are involved, then engineering faculty have a natural advantage over other disciplines. Furthermore, engineering faculty have shown more willingness to take risks in discipline-oriented research than their colleagues in the sciences. Stimulation of meaningful interests in pedagogical issues is essential.

Improving Materials/Resource Sharing

Many believe that improving the quality and dissemination of materials, i.e., resource sharing, is the most important problem. Individuals working alone rarely have the tenacity or resources to sustain the effort necessary to produce high-quality course materials in modern media. Small instructional teams, including talented graduate students, are more likely to succeed.

> If means could be found in the future to permit the sustained development of the teaching materials, the "software," of educational technology, one of the principal problems of the field might be solved. It is trite but true to say that the hardware of educational technology has always outrun the software; the hardware continues to do so today....A great deal of new software has been developed..., but most of it represents no more than a first-try effort by the scholars involved, with all of the imperfections that first-try efforts in education normally have.

Not widely appreciated is the fact that the
transformation of instructional material from the
conventional format of book and blackboard to one in
which the substance is conveyed to unseen students by a
variety of machines is an exceedingly demanding,
frustrating, and time-consuming task. Even determining
the kind of topics that lend themselves best to
presentation by each kind of device is a problem
requiring a good deal of experimentation, and when solved
may be successful with only certain kinds of students.
Once developed, a software program needs, but rarely
gets, an extended series of trials and tests.

Although the barriers to the extensive sharing of
materials are several, the main one is clear: the first
requirement of adoption of technology-based software is
that there be something worth adopting; not many
first-round efforts at developing software are. Software
must therefore become a great deal better than most of it
now is before it will have a chance of being actually
used very far beyond home base. To that end, foundations
and other organizations that support development work
might now consider financing fewer projects for longer
periods of time. Ten years is not too long to support a
major project to produce materials that have been tested,
revised, retested, and again revised, and to make a clear
demonstration of their effectiveness. If long-term
support for large projects is not forthcoming,
educational technology will continue to develop in the
haphazard and redundant fashion of the past. (ibid.)

Far more attention should be paid to understanding the reactions of
students to media. Creating environments for acceptance of ET by
campus students is more complex than it may appear. Systematic
exploration of the factors affecting student attitudes should be
encouraged, and the results of these studies periodically summarized
for educators. Effective ET will surely have to combine the
utilization of higher quality courseware with more knowledge about how
to solicit favorable student attitudes.

Mission-oriented organizations that involve subgroups of faculty
from several universities offer the potential of sustained external
guidance and stimulus. Consortia such as the Association for
Media-Based Continuing Education for Engineers (AMCEE) provide
assurance of continuity of effort regardless of changes in personnel at
individual institutions. Similar resource-sharing organizations might
be created to develop computer-aided design (CAD) instructional
materials for engineers, to create media for case studies of
engineering practice, to provide instructional films in professional
ethics, and to carry out mediated instructional programs overseas in
conjunction with foreign universities.

Encouraging Non-Bureaucratic Responses

Few, if any, educators expect to become rich in their work.
Financial incentives for faculty are not well developed in ET, and care
needs to be taken to ensure that a reasonable marketplace is created,
one which recognizes individual and group efforts. Perhaps equally
important to faculty are professional incentives and recognition. A
conscious effort to enhance the professional esteem of ET activities
should be a part of all programs.

Faculty generally perceive the university press as a prestigious
institution closely tied to a commitment of scholarship. Chester Kerr,
Director of the Yale University Press, is quoted in a lighthearted
moment as saying, "We publish the smallest editions at the greatest
cost, and on these we place the highest prices, and then we try to
market them to people who can least afford them. This is madness!"

Might it be possible to raise the level of faculty commitment to ET
by creating a selected number of modern ET "presses"? Rather than
monographs, these media-based publishers could specialize in the
production of high-quality courseware, integrating creative university
staffs in video and computation with master teachers and their
cohorts. Librarians could be trained to maintain central facilities on
each campus to expose students and faculty to outstanding examples of
ET. In time, these modern university "presses" could provide the
institutionalization and prestige which today's ET efforts lack.
Equally important, an entrepreneurial spirit could be wed early to what
could become authoritative outlets for creative ET work. Endowments
creating these new organizations would help assure not only initial
working capital but also needed autonomy.

Suggested Actions

A number of suggestions are included in the text in conjunction
with the discussion of a particular application of a technology. Table
7 summarizes these recommended actions together with one new
organizational concept which would involve all aspects of ET in
practice. Table 7 is an array of both on-campus and off-campus
applications which uses the vertical columns for specific applications
and horizontal rows for specific technologies/organizations. The
divisions involving "new" and "existing" are somewhat arbitrary but are
included to help differentiate the more research-oriented tasks from
those which could be undertaken as developmental implementations.

Since the primary purpose of this report is to provide a critical
evaluation of the ET literature with respect to its applications to
engineering education. The authors' suggestions as outlined in Table 7
are made throughout the report and are summarized here in the hope that
they will serve as stimuli for thoughtful consideration and, perhaps,
even action. The principle suggestions, listed in order of priority,
are:

TABLE 7

SUMMARY OF SUGGESTED ACTIONS

Technology	Organization	Existing Applications — On Campus	Existing Applications — Off Campus	New Applications — On Campus	New Applications — Off Campus
Existing Technology	Existing Organization	Build pool of knowledgeable educators using ET for local course improvement; studies of productivity and student attitude toward ET. (pp. 7; 91-93; 108-114)	Extend high quality graduate and continuing education nationwide through AMCEE. (pp. 59-62)		Increase use of personal ET in programs for minority students in grades 9-12. (pp. 9; 46-47; 65-66; 97-98)
Existing Technology	New Organization			Create prestigious centers of ET, "university video-presses," as new models for production of high quality course materials. (pp. 8-9; 56; 115) Encourage consortia to produce media for case studies instruction in engineering design and professional ethics. (pp. 11-12; 43-45) Fund twelve prototype centers for instruction in computer-aided design and manufacture. (pp. 7-8; 100-104)	
New Technology	Existing Organization	Fund an independent study of modern instrument and equipment problems of colleges of engineering (pp. 10-11; 98-99)	Test use of satellites and modern communication technology in the AMCEE task above. (pp. 9-10; 75-81; 110-111)	Initiate a forecast of the issues and public policies related to new consumer-oriented ET. (p. 11)	Undertake the negotiations and feasibility studies to make cooperative programs of postgraduate engineering education available to foreign nations by satellite. (pp. 10; 69; 116)
New Technology	New Organization	Undertake feasibility study for the creation of several regional centers of computation in engineering research. (pp. 13; 105-106)		Design new agency programs to encourage transfer of knowledge and courseware in ET. (pp. 11; 97)	

1. The number of talented individuals working with ET needs to be enlarged greatly in order to increase the impact of powerful new delivery systems.

   • Government agencies should design funding programs which encourage broad-scale, diversified development and testing of ET courseware in various media at the local course level. Although some basic instructional research in artificial intelligence and other, similar areas should be funded, major support should be given to improving local courses and to productivity studies. The purpose of these programs would be to involve many more faculty, nationwide, in meaningful ET activities.

2. The unique learning experiences provided by combining interactive computing with individual graphic displays, although rarely practiced today, should be widely available to engineering students. Courseware in computer-aided design and simulations of computer-aided manufacturing need to be created for all engineering disciplines. The colleges that pioneer in these endeavors will incur equipment costs and software development expenses. (Although the cost of equipment is currently high, it is likely to decline in the future.) To provide incentives for the immediate initiation of such programs, it may be necessary to subsidize a first generation of facilities. Follow-up federal programs also may be necessary several years later to ensure widespread availability of computer graphics equipment.

   • At least twelve prototype computer graphics centers should be funded in the next two years at selected engineering colleges. These centers would serve as regional models for the organization and operation of interdisciplinary facilities, as clearinghouses for vendors and educators, and as developers of outreach materials for engineering educators nationwide. External funding of these pioneering centers might require one-third to one-quarter local matching funds. A second round of facility grants to ensure the general availability of computer graphic equipment might involve as much as a 50 percent match by colleges and universities.

3. Videopublishing gives the university a distinctly new opportunity to serve the practicing professional. New organizations are needed to undertake this task. These new university "videopresses" would bring together the human resources: master teachers; manuscript editors; video production staffs; and computer software experts. All of the marketing and distribution skills of the traditional publishing house are necessary. Early efforts in videopublishing should provide visible models which combine both the scholarly prestige and the entrepreneurial spirit of the traditional university presses.

   • Several university videopresses should be endowed at universities having both a strong commitment to continuing education of professionals and the media expertise to set high standards of quality. These new enterprises would provide a creative outlet for faculty everywhere and encourage the development of modern instructional programs under the guidance of skilled staff.

4. Modern communications technologies one day may make extensive resource sharing a reality in higher education. Early efforts should focus on non-threatening domains in order to elicit maximum faculty cooperation. The AMCEE consortium brings together the resources of 22 universities which have major investments in regional ITV systems designed to provide both graduate and continuing education programs to engineers at their job sites. New communications technologies could be introduced into universities most effectively through mission-oriented activities such as those proposed by AMCEE.

- An operational plan to test the cost effectiveness of communications satellites should be funded to provide engineers with the following educational services at their job sites: national delivery of graduate credit courses in a coordinated program initially involving 10 AMCEE universities; delivery of continuing education short courses; and teleconferencing between originating sites to provide for direct faculty exchanges, special seminars, and technical meetings. Studies should be undertaken to involve ethnic minority colleges of engineering in activities of their choosing.

5. Technology exchange with foreign nations wishing to provide opportunities for engineering postgraduate study in the United States could be accomplished by means of satellite interconnections and cooperative arrangements between AMCEE colleges and foreign universities.

If satellites are used to extend U.S. engineering postgraduate education overseas, the keyword is cooperation. The details of the operations need to be negotiated with foreign educators and officials to ensure that the organizational configuration, the academic programs offered, and the assignment of academic responsibilities are distributed in a mutually agreed upon manner. Fuller (1978) argues that higher education might well be a major U.S. export industry in the future because America enjoys the opportunity of a lower real economic cost due to its existing institutions and its leadership in communications and scientific research. The preliminary studies conducted by the Association for Media-Based Continuing Education for Engineers (AMCEE) show such operations to be technically feasible. The advantages of offering high-quality educational opportunities in the homeland of the student warrant the investment necessary to employ modern communications technology as the backbone of the system.

- Post-graduate study programs offered by U.S. engineering colleges might be transmitted overseas via satellite. The potential advantages of high-quality educational opportunities available in the homeland of the student may warrant the investment necessary to employ modern communications technology.

6. Campus instructional laboratories are rarely equipped with the powerful new measurement instruments now found in industrial practice. University equipment budgets have not kept pace with the emergence of modern devices, and this problem is becoming more acute each year.

- An in-depth study of the equipment problems of colleges of engineering should be undertaken, perhaps by an industrial team sponsored by the National Research Council. Recommendations might include government incentives to industry, as well as emergency programs to overcome what has become a massive problem of hardware acquisition.

7. The decentralization of instructional computing appears inevitable. This transition will bring many new problems in funding and operations to campuses; it also will bring unparalleled opportunities to integrate computing into the students' experience.

- Federal agencies should design a number of new programs to expedite the transition to decentralized computing. These diverse efforts might include sponsorship of the following: consumers' unions to evaluate machines and courseware; visiting lectureships; workshops and summer institutes; and media-based, packaged, short courses for in-service training of teachers.

8. The case study method of instruction is gaining popularity in engineering as an effective way of bringing practical design problems into the undergraduate curriculum. Television or films have been shown to add realism and a stimulating emotional dimension to an otherwise highly abstract instructional program. However, very little media is now in use in engineering instruction.

- Foundations should explore the creation of working consortia or nonprofit organizations to produce high quality films and videotapes in support of case study instruction, especially in engineering design and in professional ethics.

9. ET has made possible engineering-related programs for students in both rural and inner-city high schools. Films produced by industry that give an orientation to engineering, introductory computer courses delivered by videotape, hand-held calculators, and personal computers all have been employed successfully in gaining the interest of ethnic minority students. More effective and universal programs now might be planned based on the experience gained to date.

- The use of ET in attracting, motivating, and preparing ethnic minority students and others who are educationally disadvantaged in grades 9 through 12 should be extended. A few university-based centers could supply materials and information to the many programs which are now sponsored by businessmen and educators regionally.

10. Decentralization of instructional computing may preclude the upgrading of university central computing facilities. University-based researchers may find it difficult to participate in the powerful advances being made in super computers.

- The National Academy of Engineering (NAE) should sponsor a feasibility study on the creation of several regional computation centers for engineering research.

11. The rush to create a consumers' market in ET will probably have a profound impact on learners of all ages. Yet, this literature survey uncovered no systematic study of the implications of this development, nor were articles found that address the issue of how educators and schools may react.

- The NAE should update its 1974 study on issues and public policies in ET in the light of current trends and forecasts in hardware delivery systems.

REFERENCES

Adams, J.A. and Rogers, D.F., "Computers," Ch. 7 in Grayson, L.P. and
    Biedenbach, J.M., Teaching Aids in the College Classroom, American
    Society for Engineering Education, Washington (1975).
Adams, J.A., "A Big Leap Forward for Computer Based Learning in the
    U.K.," Office of Naval Research, European Scientific, Notes, ONBR
    London, ESN 32-7 (July 31, 1978).
Alden, J.D., "Opportunities for Engineering Graduates," Engineering
    Education, 64, pp. 493-497 (April, 1974).
Alterman, D.L., Appel, L.R., and Murphy, R.T., "PLATO and TICCIT: An
    Evaluation of CAI in the Community College," Educational
    Technology, XVIII, in 4, pp. 40-45; plus responses from producers,
    pp. 45-46 (April, 1978).
Anderson, R.M., "Evaluation of Graduate Engineering Education by
    Television at Purdue University," Proceedings of IEEE, 66, No. 8,
    pp. 918-926 (August, 1978).
Baldwin, L.V., Collias, A.J., Davis, C.M., and Schmaling, G., Workshop
    on Continuing Education for Engineers at Midcareer, Colorado State
    University, Fort Collins, p. VIII-3 (August, 1974).
Baldwin, L.V. and Davis, P.N., "Videobased Graduate Education for
    Part-Time Students Off-Campus," Scienza & Tecnica '75, Milano,
    Italy (1975).
Barile, R.G., Hauze, R.N., and Wankat, P.C., "TV Taping of Laboratory
    Oral Reports," Proceedings of ASEE/IEEE Frontiers in Education
    Conference (1977), United Engineering Center, New York (1974).
Bartolini, R.A., Bell, A.E., Flory, R.E., Lurie, M., and Spong, F.W.,
    "Optical Disk Systems Emerge," IEEE Spectrum, 15, No. 8, pp. 20-28
    (August, 1978).
Bell, J.M. and Brenchley, D.L., "Engineering Case Study Approach for
    Studying Community Problems," Preprint from Event 2560, ASEE Annual
    Meeting, Texas Technical University, Lubbock (June, 1972).
Bigeleisen, J. (Chairman), "The Proposed National Resource for
    Computation in Chemistry: A User-Oriented Facility," Office of
    Chemistry and Chemical Technology, National Research Council,
    Washington, D.C. (1975).

Bloom, B.S. (ed.), Taxonomy of Educational Objectives: Handbook 1: The Cognitive Domain, Wiley, New York (1956).

Blum, R. (ed.), Conference Proceedings: Computers in Undergraduate Science Education, Commission on College Physics, College Park, Maryland (1971).

Bork, A., "Learning, Computers, and Pictures," Technological Horizons in Education Journal, 1, No. 5, pp. 6-13 (November, 1974).

Bork A., "Learning Through Graphics," in Sec. 5, Seidel, R.J. and Rubin, M., Computers and Communication: Implications for Education, Academic Press, Inc., New York (1977).

Bowen, C.G., "The University as Videopublisher of Last Resort," Cable Television and the University, EDUCOM, Princeton (1974).

Braun, L., "Microcomputers and Video Disc Systems: Magic Lamps for Educators?" Report to N.I.E., National Coordinating Center for Curriculum Development, State University of New York at Stony Brook (1977).

Britton, C.C. and Schweizer, H.H., "Freshman Engineering at Colorado State," Engineering Education, 65, No. 2, pp. 162-165 (November, 1974).

Brumley, W., Department of Mathematics, Colorado State University; personal communication (September, 1978).

Buchanan, P., "New Hampshires' Populist of the Right," nationally syndicated column, "The Dividing Line," Chicago Tribune-N.Y. Times Syndicate, Inc. (September, 1978).

Buchnell, D.D. and Allen, D.W. (eds.), The Computer in American Education, John Wiley & Sons, Inc., New York (1967).

Bugliarello, G., et al., "Issues and Public Policies in Educational Technology," Report of N.A.E. Advisory Committee, Lexington Books, D. C. Heath & Co., Lexington, Massachusetts (1974).

Bulkeley, P.Z., (ed.), "Authentic Involvement in Interdisciplinary Design," Proceedings of the Third Conference on Engineering Design Education, Carnegie Institute of Technology, Pittsburgh, Pennsylvania (June, 1965).

Business Week, "Texas Instruments Shows U.S. Business How to Survive in the 1980's," Number 2552, pp. 66-92 (September 18, 1978).

Carnegie Commission on Higher Education, The Fourth Revolution: Instructional Technology in Higher Education, McGraw-Hill, New York (1972).

Carpenter, C.R., "Instructional Television Research," Report No. 2, Pennsylvania State University, University Park (1958).

Chemical and Engineering News, 53, "Engineering Society Tackles Age Bias," p. 7 (September 22, 1975).

Cohen, K.C. (ed.), "Proceedings of the First National Workshop on Energy Efficiency Education Through Technology Transfer," Division of Power Systems, U.S. Department of Energy (December, 1977). (Available from the Editor, Room 9-369, Massachusetts Institute of Technology).

Cohen, K.C., "Project PROCEED: A Traditional and Innovative Approach to Continuing Engineering Education," Preprint, ASEE Annual Meeting, University of British Columbia, Vancouver, Canada (June, 1978).

Committee on Satellite Communications of the Space Applications Board, "Federal Research and Development for Satellite Communications," National Research Council, National Academy of Sciences, Washington, D.C. (1977).

CONDUIT, Abstracts and Reviews of Tested Curriculum Materials, University of Iowa, Iowa City (Spring, 1977).

CONDUIT, Computers in Undergraduate Teaching: State of the Art Report for Selected Disciplines, University of Iowa, Iowa City (1977).

Control Data Education Co., Courseware Catalog, Educational Services of Control Data Corporation, Minneapolis-St. Paul (January, 1978).

Davis, C.M. and Gunderson, N.O., "Description of a Successful Joint Venture in ITV-Based Continuing Education," Workshop on Continuing Education for Engineers at Midcareer, Colorado State University, Fort Collins (August, 1974).

Deardorff, J.W., "A Numerical Study of Three-Dimensional Turbulent Channel Flow at Large Reynolds Numbers," Journal of Fluid Mechanics, 41, pp. 453-480 (1970).

Denk, J.R., "Instructional Computing Support for Higher Education," Conference of Computer Applications in Instruction for College and University Executives, IBM, San Jose, Calif. (July 7-9, 1976).

Diehl, M.H., "Use of Hand-Held Calculator in Algebra I Classes in Chicago Public Schools: June 1977 - June 1978," National Coordinating Center for Curriculum Development, State University of New York at Stony Brook (September, 1978).

Down, K.S., "The Stanford Instructional TV Network: A Survey of Its Students," Engineering Education, 66, pp. 762-763 (April, 1976).

Dwyer, T. and Sweer, L., "The Cybernetic Crayon: A Low Cost Approach to Human Interaction with Color Graphics," Byte, 1, No. 12 (December, 1976).

Educational Policy Research Center, Instructional Television: A Comparative Study of Satellite and Other Delivery Systems, Syracuse Research Corporation, Syracuse, New York (November, 1976).

Eide, A., "Educational Television," paper presented at ASEE Annual Meeting (1971).

Eide, A., "Instructional Modules with Cassette Television," paper presented at ASEE Annual Meeting (1974).

Feinstein, W., Bell Labs, 600 Mountain Avenue, Office No. 3B-337, Murray Hill, New Jersey, personal communication (September, 1978).

Flanagan, D. (ed.), Microelectronics, W. H. Freeman & Co., San Francisco (September, 1977).

Florman, S., The Existential Pleasures of Engineering, St. Martins Press, Inc., New York (1975).

Fuller, A.B., "The Educationalization of America," The Chroncile of Higher Education, XVIII, No. 8, p. 40 (October 28, 1978).

Gibbons, J.F., Kincheloe, W.R., and Down, K.S., "Tutored Videotape Instruction: A New Use of Electronics Media in Education," Science, 195, pp. 1,139-41,146 (March, 1977).

Gilbert, T.L., Lykos, P., and Wahl, A.C. (eds.), "Planning a National Center for Large Scale Computation in Chemistry Research," Argonne National Laboratory and Argonne Universities Association, ANL-8085 (June, 1974).

Haggerty, P.E., "Individualized Instruction and Productivity in Education," Ch. 1 in Grayson, L.P. and Biedenbach, J.S. (eds.), Individualized Instruction in Engineering Education, ASEE Monogram Series (May, 1974).

Hamblen, J.W., "Academic and Administrative Computing: Where Are We?" EDUCOM Bulletin, 12, 1, pp. 2-7 (Spring, 1977).

Hamblen, J.W., Department of Computer Science, University of Missouri-Rolla; personal communication (September 29, 1978).

Hamblen, J.W. and Landis, C.P., (eds.), The Fourth Inventory of Computers in Higher Education, EDUCOM Series in Computing and Telecommunications in Higher Education, No. 4, Princeton (1980).

Hamblin, W.H., "Dilemmas in Legal Ethics," Catalog of Videotape Programs, Consortium for Professional Education, American Bar Association, 115 East 60th St., Chicago, Illinois 60637 (July, 1978).

Hartley, J., "Programmed Instruction 1954-74: A Review," Programmed Learning and Educational Technology, 11, No. 6, (November, 1974).

Hawkridge, D.G., "Media Taxonomies and Media Selection," Milton Keynes, England (mimeo, not dated).

Hawkridge, D.G., "Problems in Implementing Computer Managed Learning," British Journal of Educational Technology, 1, No. 5, pp. 31-43 (January, 1976).

Hayman, R.W. and Lord, W., "A Technology-Based Educational System Using Computer Management," Educational Technology, XII, No. 12, pp. 43-52 (December, 1972).

Hayman, R.W. and Levin, H., "Economic Analysis and Historical Summary of Educational Technology Costs," Appendix C of Melmed, A. (ed.), Productivity and Efficiency in Education, Federal Council on Science and Technology, Washington, D.C. (1973).

Heuston, D.H., "The Promise and Inevitability of the Videodisc in Education," Report to N.I.E., WICAT, Inc., Orem, Utah (September, 1977).

Holman, J.P., Department of Mechnical Engineering, Southern Methodist University, personal communication (1977).

Holmes, R., Dean of Engineering, General Motors Institute, Flint, Michigan, personal communication (1978).

Hooper, R., "Making Claims for Computers," International Journal of Mathematics, Education, Science, and Technology, 5, pp. 359-368 (1974).

Jamison, D., Suppes, P., and Wells, S., "The Effectiveness of Alternative Instructional Media: A Survey," Review of Educational Research, 44, No. 1, pp. 1-68 (Winter, 1974).

Keller, F.R. and Koen, B.V., "The Personalized System of Instruction: State of the Art 1976," Section 3, University of Texas at Austin (1976).

Kenyon, R., Dean of Engineering, Rochester Institute of Technology, Rochester, New York, personal communication (September, 1978).

Klus, J.P. and Jones, J.A., Engineers Involved in Continuing Education: A Survey Analysis, ASEE Monogram, Washington, D.C. (March, 1975).

Koen, B.V., "Teaching Engineering Design by Authentic Design," Proceedings of Joint Automatic Controls Conference, Purdue University, West Lafayette, Indiana (1976).

Koerner, J.D., "The Present and the Future in Educational Technology," Alfred P. Sloan Foundation, New York (May, 1977).

Lauer, B.E. (ed.), THE Catalog, 4 volumes, 146 Fourteenth St., Boulder, Colorado 80303 (1978).

Lipson, J.I., "Conditions for Progress in Instructional Technology," Sec. 3 in Seidel, R.J. and Rubin, M.L., Computers and Communications: Implications for Education, pp. 221-229, Academic Press, Inc., New York (1977).

Loomis, H.H., Jr. and Brandt, H., "Television as a Tool in Engineering Education," IEEE Transactions on Education, E6, Issue 2, pp. 101-109 (May, 1973).

Luehrmann, A., "Dartmouth Project COEXIST," Proceedings on Computers in Undergraduates Curricula, Dartmouth College, Hanover, New Hampshire, p. 2 (1971).

Lumsdale, A.A. and Glaser, R., "Teaching Machines and Programmed Learning: A Source Book," Department of Audiovisual Instruction, National Education Association, Washington, D.C. (1960).

Lykos, Peter, "E^3 - Role of Computer," Association for Computing Machinery, SIGCUE Bulletin, 9, No. 1, pp. 28-29 (January, 1975).

Lykos, P., (ed.), Minicomputers and Large Scale Computations, American Chemical Society (ACS) Symposium Series No. 57, ACS, Washington, D.C. (1977).

Lykos, P., (ed.), "Proceedings of a Conference on the Use of Media-Based Materials by Professional Societies in Continuing Education," Association for Media-Based Continuing Education for Engineers, Georgia Institute of Technology, Atlanta, Georgia 30332 (October, 1978a).

Lykos, P., (ed.), Computer Modeling of Matter, American Chemical Society (ACS) Symposium Series No. 86, ACS, Washington, D.C. (1978b).

Magidson, E.M., "Student Assessment of PLATO: What Students Like and Dislike About CAI," Educational Technology, XVIII, No. 8, pp. 15-18 (August, 1978).

Maxwell, L.M., "CSU Educational Media: Part III; Co-Tie - Cooperation Among Colleges," Technological Horizons in Education Journal, 5, No. 3, pp. 36-38 (May/June, 1978).

McCosh, R.B., "Television Assisted Instruction in Accounting," Journal of Business Education, XLV, No. 7, pp. 274-276 (1970).

McCosh, R.B., personal communication, Colorado State University, Fort Collins (September, 1978).

Melmed, A. (ed.), "Productivity and Efficiency in Education," Federal Council on Science and Technology, Washington, D.C. (1973).

Merrill, M.D. (ed.), Instructional Design: Readings, Prentice-Hall, Inc., Englewood Cliffs, New Jersey (1971).

Miller, D.C. and Baldwin, L.V., "Use of Television for Presentations," Ch. 5 in Grayson, L.P. and Biedenbach, J.M. (eds.), Teaching Aids in the College Classroom, ASEE, Washington, D.C. (1975).

Mitzel, H.E. (ed.), Conference Proceedings: An Examination of the Short-Range Potential of Computer-Managed Instruction, Pennsylvania State University, Report on NIE Grant No. C-74-0091 (November, 1974).

Molnar, A.R., "National Policy Toward Technological Innovation and Academic Computing," National Science Foundation Manuscript, Washington, D.C. (1977).

Morris, A.J., Down, K.S., Munushian, J., McGhie, L.F., Rubenstein, R., and Hike, R.C., "Final Report on Cost Effectiveness of Continuing Engineering Studies by Television," CES Division, American Society of Engineering Education, Washington, D.C. (May, 1974).

Morris, A., et al., "The Return on Investment in Continuing Education of Engineers," Final Report on NSF Grant EPP-75-21587, Genesys Systems, Inc., Palo Alto, Calif. (May, 1978).

National Institute of Education, "Conference on Educational Applications of Satellites," Arlington, Virginia, National Institute of Education, Washington, D.C. (February, 1977).

Neidt, C.O., "Final Report: Project Colorado CO-TIE," Prepared under NSF Grant GY 5305, Colorado State University, Fort Collins (1970).

Neidt, C.O. and Baldwin, L.V., "The Use of Videotape for Teaching In-Plant Graduate Engineering Courses," Adult Education, XX, No. 3, pp. 154-167 (1970).

Oliver, B.M., "The Role of Microelectronics in Instrumentation and Control: Ch. 8, in Flanagan, D. (ed.), Microelectronics, W. H. Freeman & Co., San Francisco (1977).

Papert, S., "A Learning Environment for Children," in Sec. 4, Seidel, R.J. and Rubin, M.L. (eds.), Computers and Communications: Implications for Education, pp. 271-278, Academic Press, Inc., New York (1977).

Pask, G. and Lewis, B., "Teaching Strategies: A Systems Approach," in Unit 9 of The Curriculum: Context, Design and Development, Open University, United Kingdom (1972).

Perlberg, A. and O'Bryant, D.C., "Videotaping and Microteaching Techniques to Improve Engineering Instruction," Engineering Education, 60, pp. 741-744 (March, 1970).

Pettit, J. and Hawkins, W. (eds.), "Final Report: Goals of Engineering Education," Journal of Engineering Education, 369-446 (January 1968).

Pollask, R.A., "Computer Augmented Video Education: An Overview," Proceedings of the Ninth Conference on Computers in Undergraduate Curricula, Library of Congress Card No. 74-10711 (1978).

President's Science Advisory Committee, Committees in Higher Education, U.S. Government Printing Office, Washington D. C. (1967).

Prestia, J.V., "Computer Augmented Video Education in Troublesome areas of Chemistry," Proceedings of the Ninth Conference on Computers in Under-Graduate Curricula, Library of Congress Card No. 74-10700 (1978).

Pritsker, A. and Allen, B., GASP-IV: Simulation Language, John Wiley & Sons, New York (1974).

Rahman, A. and Stillinger, S.H., "Molecular Dynamics Study of Liquid Water," Journal of Chemical Physics, 55, pp. 3,336-3,359 (1971).

Rivers, R.A., "Age Discrimination Patterns in Engineering Employment," in The E/E at Mid-Career - Prospects and Problems, The Institute of Electrical and Electronic Engineers, Inc., Washington, D.C. (1975).

Rogers, J.L., "The Russians Are Learning," Audio-Visual Communication (April, 1974).

Rogers, J.L., "Moving From Broadcast to Videotape in a University-Based Instructional TV Network," Proceedings of ASEE College Industry Education Conference, San Diego (January, 1978), Washington, D.C., 1978.

Rosauer, E.A., "Electron Microscopy via Television," Engineering Education, 60, p. 710 (March, 1970).

Rosenstein, A.B., "Modeling, Analysis, Synthesis, Optimization, and Decision Making in Engineering Curricula," DEP-2-68, Report of Department of Engineering, University of California in Los Angeles (1968).

Rothenberg, D. and Morgan, R.P., "Case Studies of Innovation in the Educational Service Sector," Center for Development Technology, Washington University, St. Louis (July, 1975).

Salloway, N., "Video at MIT: A Progress Report," Center for Advanced Engineering Study, Massachusetts Institute of Technology, Cambridge (May, 1974).

Sanders, H.J., "Continuing Education: The Intensified Effort to Keep Up To Date," Chemical and Engineering News, pp. 18-27, 26-38 (May 13 and 20, 1974).

Schmaling, G.P., "Status of Video Based Graduate Engineering Education in the United States," Workshop on Continuing Education for Engineering at Mid-Career, Colorado State University, Fort Collins, pp. 1-58 (August, 1974).

Schneider, E.W., "Applications of Videodisc Technology to Individualize Instruction," Session 5, in Seidel, R.J. and Rubin, M., Computers and Communications: Implications for Education, pp. 313-326, Academic Press, Inc., New York (1977).

Schramm, W., (ed.), Quality in Instructional Television, The University Press of Hawaii (1972).

Schramm, W., Big Media, Little Media: Tools and Technologies for Instruction, Sage Publications, Inc., Beverly Hills, California (1977).

Science, "Computer Films: Adding an Extra Dimension to Research," 200, pp. 749-752 (May 19, 1978).

Scott, K.E., Peura, R.A., and Demetry, J.S., "The W.P.I. Plan: A Case Study," Ch. 10 in Grayson, L.P. and Biedenbach, J.M. (eds.), Individualized Instruction in Engineering Education, ASEE Monogram Series, Washington, D.C. (May, 1974).

Scott, K.E., "Self-Paced Laboratory Modules to Support Projects and Independent Study," Event 3272 Preprint, 86th Annual Meeting of ASEE, University of British Columbia, Vancouver (1978).

Seidel, R.J. and Rubin, M., Computers and Communication: Implications for Education, Academic Press, Inc., New York (1977).

Seltzer, Norman, Scientific and Engineering Manpower Redefined: 1972 Postcensual Survey of Professional Scientific and Technical

Manpower; Vol. 1 - Demographic, Educational and Professional Characteristics, NSF 75-313 (May, 1975); Vol. 2 - Employment Characteristics, NSF 76-323 (1976); Vol. 3, Geographic, NSF-76-33 National Science Foundation, Washington, D.C. (1976).

Shapiro, A., et al., Illustrated Experiments in Fluid Mechanics, M.I.T. Press, Cambridge, Massachusetts (1972).

Sjogren, D., Baldwin, L., Jacobson, L., and Birkeland, D., "Studies on the Use of Extramural Videopublished Materials in Continuing Education,: Final Report on NSF Grant HES 75-19854, Colorado State University, Fort Collins (August, 1976).

Skinner, B.F., "The Science of Learning and the Art of Teaching," Harvard Educational Review, Cambridge, Massachusetts, 24, 2 (1954).

Smith, E., "TV or Not TV? That's the Question," Engineering Education, 64, pp. 505-506 (April, 1974).

Starke, J.W., "Will Teachers Be the Next Dodo Birds," Engineering Education, 63, No. 3, pp. 196-198 (1972).

Stice, J.E., "The Personalized System of Instruction (PSI): The Keller Plan Applied in Engineering Education," Bureau of Engineering Teaching, Bulletin, 4, University of Texas at Austin (1971).

Strover, S., "Curriculum-Sharing Via Satellite, Final Report on the Stanford-Carleton-NASA-Ames CTS Demonstration," Institute for Communication Research, Stanford Unversity, Stanford, California (February, 1978).

Stutzman, W.L. and Grigsby, L.L., "A Multimedia Approach to Remote Classroom Instruction," Engineering Education, 63, pp. 119-123 (November, 1973).

Sugarman, R., "A Second Chance for Computer-Aided Instruction," IEEE Spectrum, 15, pp. 29-37 (August, 1978).

Suydam, M.N., "Periodic Newsletter," Calculator Information Center, 1200 Chambers Road, Columbus, Ohio 45212 (1978).

Tickton, S. (ed.), To Improve Learning, Report by the U.S. Commission on Instructional Technology, Bowker Publishing, New York (1970).

Tribus, M., "The Three Faces of Technology and the Implications for Engineering Education," R.P. Davis Memorial Address, West Virginia University (March 17, 1975).

Vesper, K.H. and Adams, J.L., "Evaluating Learning from the Case Methods," Engineering Education, 59, pp. 104-106 (October, 1969).

Vesper, K.H. and Adams, J.L., "Teaching Objectives, Style and Effect with the Case Method," Engineering Education, 61, pp. 831-833 (April, 1971).

Wales, C.E. and Stager, R.A., "The Design of an Educational System," Engineering Education, 62, 456-59, 488, (February, 1972).

Ward, J.C., "Cable Television Hardware: The State of the Art," Proceedings of the Conference on Cable Television and the University, EDUCOM, P.O. Box 364, Princeton, New Jersey (January, 1974).

Ward, R.C. and Maxwell, L.M., "HI-TIE: The University, the High School and Engineering," Engineering Education, 64, No. 4, pp. 325-328 (January, 1975).

Whitney, T.M., "Compact Computers for the 1980's," in Seidel, R.J., and Rubin, M. (eds.), Computers and Communication: Implications for Education, Academic Press, Inc., New York (1977).

Willey, L.V. Jr., "Computers and Instructional Productivity," a Professional Report, International Business Machines Corporation, Bethesda, Maryland (May, 1975).

Wozny, M.J., "Interactive Computer Graphics for Engineering Education," Professional Engineering, 48, No. 6, pp. 14-18 (June, 1978).

Zinn, K.L., "Instructional Uses of Computers in Higher Education," Ch. 5 in Hamblen, J.W. (ed.), The Fourth Inventory of Computers in Higher Education, EDUCOM Series in Computing, No. 4 (1980).

ACKNOWLEDGMENTS

Throughout this report the authors have cited many authorities and provided extensive references to enhance its utility. Appreciation is expressed to all, with specific acknowledgment of the permissions received for reprinting certain tables, figures, and text.

Figures 1 and 3. Reproduced with permission of R. W. Hayman, from page 26 of the 1973 Hayman/Levin paper. (See References.)

Figure 2. Reproduced with permission of Billy V. Koen from the 1976 Keller/Koen paper. (See References.)

Figure 7. Reproduced from the 1977 Whitney paper. (See References.)

Figure 8, Table 5, and Table 6. Reproduced with permission of John W. Hamblen. (See References.)

Appendix A. Mrs. Iris M. Wiley, Executive Editor, The University Press of Hawaii approved reprint of two pages from a chapter by W. Schramm, "What Research Says About ITV," from Quality in Instructional Television, an East-West Center book copyright 1972, The University Press of Hawaii.

Appendix B. Reprinted with permission of the author.

Appendix C. Ms. Carolyn P. Landis, Secretary to the Corporation, Interuniversity Communications Council, Inc., authorized this reprint of C. B. Bowen's paper, "The University as Videopublisher of Last Resort," from the proceedings, CABLE TELEVISION AND THE UNIVERSITY (1974). EDUCOM is the publisher. The ERIC document number is ED 093 378.

Appendix D. "A Second Chance for Computer-Aided Instruction," by Robert Sugarman is reprinted from IEEE SPECTRUM, August 1978, vol. 15, no. 8, pp. 29-37, with the permission of IEEE.

APPENDIXES

Each of the following four appendixes expands on an important facet of the role of modern technology in engineering education.

Appendix A: A recognized authority on instructional media, Wilbur Schramm, summarizes what he gleaned from a review of many research studies of instructional television (ITV). Schramm concentrates on the way the subject matter is presented and the instructional strategies of ITV, i.e., what the teacher and the producer can do within the program to help viewers learn.

Appendix B: Productivity is an economic concept often used by the makers of public policy. Productivity may also be the most flexible framework for evaluating what ET does when it is applied at the local level.
In 1974, Lawrence V. Willey, Jr., studied operational applications of computing in instruction. The purpose of the inquiry was to define instructional productivity in practical terms and to identify examples in which computing demonstrably improved instructional productivity. This concept is not well understood by educators. Perhaps, these examples will help.

Appendix C is an enjoyable account of the history of textbooks, the first education technology (ET). Viewed in this context, today's educator is more flexible toward ET than usually thought.

Appendix D: IEEE Associate Editor, Robert Sugarman, surveys the status of computer-aided instruction (CAI) in the August, 1978, issue of SPECTRUM. He gives a balanced view of past problems and successes, and focuses on the possible impact of the new "intelligent videodisc."

APPENDIX A
WHAT RESEARCH SAYS ABOUT ITV
W. Schramm

Quality in Instructional Television
The University Press of Hawaii (1972)

"Recall some of the details in which complexity, fanciness, costliness of programming have been shown not necessarily to contribute to learning:

-- Color seems not to increase learning unless color is what is to be learned or unless it is the best means available to code some discriminations that are to be learned.
-- A big screen seems to be of no advantage to learning if the ordinary television screen can be seen clearly enough to pick out the details that are to be learned.
-- Students like a "talkback" system, but seem to learn no more with it than without it.
-- Visual embellishments do not usually help learning unless (like directional arrows) they can help organize content that is not inherently well organized or (like animation) help a viewer to understand a process or concept that is very hard to understand without such simplification. In other words, visual embellishments per se are not especially useful in instructional material.
-- No advantage has been demonstrated for existing three-dimensional projection.
-- No learning advantage has been demonstrated for "professional" or "artistic" production techniques such as dollying rather than cutting, key rather than flat lighting, dissolves, wipes, fades, etc.
-- Eye contact seems not to contribute to learning, although it may contribute to persuasion.
-- There is very little evidence that narrative presentation ordinarily has any learning advantage over expository or that adding humor adds to learning effect.

Remember that we are talking about learning, not liking. Some of these complexities may cause a student to like a program better, and in special cases any of the special treatments we have mentioned may contribute also to learning. But for the most part, the research encourages us toward a simple rather than a complex or fancy style.

Another part of the literature also has implications for simplicity and economy. This is the group of experiments that casts doubt on the greater effectiveness of two channels over one in presenting essentially redundant material. This research suggests that the auditory channel may be more effective with simple than with complex material, whereas the visual is likely to be more effective than the auditory with complex material; and that there seems to be little learning advantage for an audiovisual treatment over a visual one as long as the program is carrying as much information as the student can process and as long as the two channels are basically carrying the same information.

These later experiments deserve the consideration of educators and instructional broadcasters. They challenge us to analyze more carefully the uses of ITV that do promise a reliable advantage over a single channel, and the most effective ways we can go about presenting non-redundant information on the two channels. Furthermore, they challenge us to reconsider the tasks for which we can efficiently use the less expensive single-channel media -- radio, slides, filmstrips, sound tape, or even (pardon the word!) print -- in place of more expensive sound films and television, which in many cases may have less advantage than we had thought.

The chief positive guideline that emerges from the research is the usefulness of active student participation. Concerning that we have been able to report impressively consistent results. Participation may be overt or covert; spoken or written or done through practice with a model or a device; button pushing or asking or answering questions, or finishing what the instructor has begun to say. Different forms are more effective in different situations. Whatever the way in which students are encouraged to practice the desired responses, in most cases this activity is more effective if the students are given immediate knowledge of results -- that is, told whether their responses are correct.

There are a number of minor points in the literature that will be of interest to practitioners: when subjective camera angle is of aid to learning, the useful number of repetitions, and the usefulness of rest breaks are three that occur to me at the moment. It is unfortunate that research has not found out more in a general way about some of the big questions, like the organization of instructional television programs and the qualities of an effective ITV teacher. In general the literature is not at a very high level of generality. Findings must always be applied in terms of the nature of the instructional task, the situation, and the learners. And we are still at a stage when it pays richly to try out pilot programs and test the effectiveness at least of a sample of ongoing programs against the criterion they are expected to reach.

But at least two straightforward guidelines stand out from the research papers we have reviewed. Effective television can be kept as simple as possible, except where some complexity is clearly required for one task or another; students will learn more if they are kept actively participating in the teaching-learning process. Simple television: active students."

APPENDIX B

INQUIRY REPORT: COMPUTERS AND INSTRUCTIONAL PRODUCTIVITY

Lawrence V. Willey , Jr.
International Business Machines Corporation
Bethesda, Maryland
May 1, 1975

Details about examples of improved instructional productivity due to
the use of computer technology:

1. Robert L. Bishop
    Department of Journalism
    University of Michigan
    Ann Arbor , Michigan

    Application: Journalism Computer Assisted Instruction

    Inputs: Computer programs for specific exercises, general
                    stylistic analyses, spelling checks, and storing of
                    performance data. A programmed book for
                    self-instruction. Video tapes on writing,
                    interviewing, reporting on public opinion polls,
                    and laws of libel.

    Production: Student articles analyzed by computer for key words
                    or phrases, accuracy checks, and some libel
                    exposures. In addition, sentence/paragraph lengths
                    and use of passive verbs, descriptive adverbs, and
                    wordy sentences are evaluated. Comments are
                    printed out about each sentence (if applicable).
                    Students rewrite articles on the basis of comments.

    Outputs: Student time saving, i.e., 14 weeks to complete
                    course with JCAI compared to 20-25 weeks before
                    JCAI. Subsequent student performance, i.e.,
                    students who completed prerequisite journalism
                    course with JCAI scored 1/2 grade point higher in
                    subsequent writing course than students who had
                    journalism course without JCAI. Avoidance of cost
                    increases, i.e., enrollment had been doubled with
                    no additional faculty (computing costs $10 per
                    student/semester in comparison with $1500 for each

101

teaching assistant and $4400 for each faculty member assigned to the course). Faculty efficiency, i.e., faculty correct 1/2 to 1/3 less papers and devote time saved to helping students on an individual basis.

Additional
Materials: Available from the Center for Research on Learning and Teaching, University of Michigan, 109 East Main Street, Ann Arbor, Michigan 48104.

2. William A. Shrode
    College of Business
    Florida State University
    Tallahassee, Florida

    Application: Business Data Processing

    Inputs: Computer programs for concept drills and quizzes, programming language skills, and banks of questions. Reorganization of course and laboratory to accommodate additional students.

    Production: Students take diagnostic quizzes and drills in basic course concepts to reinforce text materials; complete exercises in programming; and use computer-generated questions to test understanding of units. Computer provides immediate evaluation/ feedback on quizzes, drills, exercises and tests and relates drills/exercises to individual needs to students.

    Outputs: Costs avoidance, i.e., course is taught with 1 1/2 less faculty members (equivalent) than would be required without computer with no significant change in student performance.

3. Jo Ann Harris Bowlsbey
    Education Department
    Carroll Hall
    Western Maryland College
    Westminster, Maryland

    Application: Computerized Vocational Information System (Based exclusively on experiences at Willowbrook High School in 1973-74)

    Inputs: Data bases of individual student information; educational institution characteristics, program requirements etc; and occupational descriptions, expectations, prerequisites, etc. Computer programs for student/counselor access and interactions with data bases.

Production: Students explore on an individual basis with terminals educational and occupational opportunities. Based on data from their past records, students examine feasibility of alternative educational and career plans. Computer relates educational and occupational information to each student's attributes.

Outputs: Increased student attendance, i.e., 133 1/3% more student contacts with guidance services in a year through computer/counselors than with counselors alone. Cost avoidance under the above conditions for "information giving" functions, i.e., $1.92 per student contact with computer compared to $12.97 per student contact with counselor.

Additional
Reference: Harris, Jo Ann, "The Computer: Guidance Tool of the Future," Journal of Counseling Psychology, 1974, Volume 21, Number 4.

4. Gerald R. Kissler
    Office of the Chancellor
    University of California Los Angeles
    Los Angeles, California

Application: LABSIM Simulation Program, 1971-1973
               (Based exclusively on experience at Washington State University)

Inputs: Computer programs for batch and interactive data generation, certain statistical procedures, and recording student work. Nine models illustrating basic psychological principles.

Production: Students select experimental designs, number of samples to be run, and values for independent variables. Computer determines values of dependent variables, means, standard deviations and t-tests. Error messages and checks of student selection of variables also provided by computer.

Outputs: Cost reduction, i.e., from conventional lab instruction of $180 to $80 for interactive simulation and $2 for batch simulation per experiment for a class of 25 students. In addition, student time was saved and types of experiments conducted were expanded with simulations.

Additional
Reference: Kissler, Gerald R., "Evaluation of Computer-Based
Laboratory Simulation Models to Teach Scientific
Research Strategies," Behavior Research Methods
and Instrumentation, 1974, Volume 6, Number 2.

5. Dana B. Main
    Department of Psychology
    University of Michigan
    Ann Arbor, Michigan

    Application: EXPER SIM Data Generator

    Inputs: Computer programs for generation and analysis of
                   data; and portable computer terminal.

    Production: Students design experiments, formulate research
                   strategies, and perform analysis of data.
                   Instructors enter variables in computer programs to
                   be used by students. Data are generated by
                   computer for student to test hypotheses, to modify
                   research strategies, and to draw conclusions.

    Outputs: Cost avoidance, i.e., per student computing costs
                   for course of $7 is less than half similar cost for
                   physical lab (without computer simulations).
                   Controlled experimental study showed EXPER SIM
                   significantly more effective for student learning
                   (as measured on local content tests) than
                   traditional class discussion/critique writing
                   approach.

6. J. Peter Williamson
    Amos Tuck School of Business
    Dartmouth College
    Hanover, New Hampshire

    Application: Business Investment Course

    Inputs: Special test on analytical theories and techniques;
                   sets of cases and problems; computer programs;
                   banks of financial data on corporation, mutual
                   funds, etc; and manuals for using programs.

    Production: Students analyze past financial performance data
                   and compile/compare portfolios. They compute
                   investment values of stock; test techniques for
                   determining stock profitability and price/earnings
                   ratios; and calculate relative merits of bond
                   purchases/sales.

Outputs:
Course content improvement, i.e., students' understanding and use of advanced techniques for analysis and problem solving (simulation, modeling, etc.). Added student efficiency in terms of greater individualization of student work; increased number and types of cases/problems completed by students and reduction in student time for routine computations. Increased student knowledge of real current investment problems rather than textbook exercises.

Additional
Materials:
Williamson, J. Peter, "Business Administration Instruction Systems: Experience at the Amos Tuck Graduate Business School." Comments for EDUCOM Spring Conference, 1973.

7. Russell V. Skavaril
    Department of Genetics
    The Ohio State University
    Columbus, Ohio

Application: Computer-Based Introductory Statistics

Inputs:
CAI modules with handouts; and computer programs for generating exercises, data analyses, statistical calculations, and student record-keeping.

Production:
Students individually complete questions in modules and analyze data in related lab work. Additional text materials, practice problems, review questions and optional quizzes can be prescribed for each student to supplement module and lab work. Student quiz scores are maintained along with instructor evaluations of students.

Outputs:
Student efficiency, i.e., students using computer-based instruction completed course in 30% less time than students using conventional lecture/laboratory approach with no significant differences in student performance on final examinations. Course content improvements: (a) all students using computer completed course materials prior to final examinatons while students using conventional instruction did not, and; (b) computer-based lab included more sets of data (both in number and type) for student analysis than conventional lab could offer.

Additional
Reference: Skavaril, Russell V., "Computer-Based Instruction
of Introductory Statistics," Journal of
Computer-Based Instruction, August, 1974, Volume 1,
Number 1.

8. Catherine E. Morgan
    Computer Assisted Instruction Program
    Montgomery County Public Schools
    Kensington, Maryland

    Application: Computer-Managed Mathematics (Geometry)

    Inputs: Special diagnostic and criterion tests. Computer
                   programs for scoring tests, prescribing
                   assignments, and keeping student records.
                   Reorganization of units into clusters to provide
                   for individualization and accommodate additional
                   students.

    Production: Students may opt to take diagnostic tests before
                   each unit for placement. Thereafter, they read
                   text material, complete related assignments, and,
                   at computer terminals, take criterion assessment
                   tests on those objectives for which they have shown
                   mastery of the prerequisites. On the basis of
                   performance, students are re-cycled to additional
                   materials on objectives not mastered or advanced to
                   the next cluster of objectives. Computer scores
                   tests, prescribes assignments, and keeps records of
                   students on individual basis.

    Outputs: Increased student attendance, i.e., 40% more
                   students have been placed in computer-managed
                   mathematics class than were assigned to
                   conventional classes with no loss in their
                   achievement. Standardized achievement test scores
                   were also significantly improved for underachieving
                   students in the computer-managed course. Personal
                   attention to students by teachers has been
                   increased significantly. Increase in class size
                   displaces cost of terminals and communication with
                   school buildings but does not cover other program
                   expenses.

9. Victor Thomas
    Newark Board of Education
    Newark, New Jersey

    Application: Arithmetic Proficiency Training Program

Inputs: Computer programs for diagnosis, practice, and testing of arithmetic skills, and for instructional management and student record keeping. Computer terminals.

Production: Students are placed individually in skill sequences based on performance on diagnostic tests. They develop new skills by completing drill exercises in small incremental steps. Mastery of specific skills is tested before students advance. Computer provides immediate feedback on students on exercises and tests. It controls assignment of exercises and tests, and compiles records for each students.

Outputs: Student attendance, i.e., average attendance rate of students in program was 96%, compared to 89% for their entire school. Standarized achievement test growth, i.e., students using APTP advanced 1.6 years in computational skills in eight months, while control group of students advanced 1.0 year during the same period. Subsequent testing showed that above test gains made by students using APTP were maintained.

10. G. C. Jernstedt
Department of Psychology
Dartmouth College
Hanover, New Hampshire

Application: Individualized Psychology Course

Inputs: Special writing and discussion assignments for students on basic course concepts. Academic assistants for evaluating student papers and discussions. Computer programs and support for maintaining individual student records and estimating future student requirements.

Production: Students individually relate basic course concepts to novels by writing a series of nine 300-word papers. Mastery of each concept is demonstrated in papers before students advance. Papers and discussions are scored by academic assistants and entered in computer. On the basis of student scores, computer provides "expectancy requirements" in terms of trials and time necessary to complete successfully remaining papers. Students receive scores and above information within 24 hours after submitting each paper.

Outputs: Student attendance, i.e., enrollment has increased
            from average of 50 to 195 students per class.
            Student efficiency, i.e., students paced their
            assignments more evenly during the course and felt
            grading was more accurate than they had experienced
            with traditional instruction. Test scores, i.e.,
            on essay exams students using computerized
            (individual) approach scored significantly higher
            than students using traditional approach.

11. Allen C. Kelley
    Department of Economics
    Duke University
    Durham, North Carolina

    Application: Individualized Economics Course
                   (Based on experiences at University of Wisconsin in
                   1971-72)

    Inputs: Student data base including aptitude and
                   achievement test scores, math background
                   information, previous record in economics, etc.
                   Survey questionnaires developed on course
                   objectives, content, etc. Computer programs for
                   scoring survey forms, applying decision rules, and
                   generating assignments/reports.

    Production: Students fill out weekly survey forms covering
                   reading materials and lectures. Reports of survey
                   forms are printed for each student, teaching
                   assistant, and instructor. Assignments are
                   suggested in student reports on individual basis.
                   Reports to teaching assistants and instructor point
                   out strengths and weaknesses for improving
                   effectiveness of instruction.

    Outputs: Test scores, i.e., students in individualized
                   course using computers scored 15% higher (average)
                   on final examinations than students in traditional
                   course (without computerized individualization)*.
                   Lower achieving students scored 19% higher on exams
                   with computer than those students without
                   computer. Follow-up testing one year later
                   confirmed that the above test gains were
                   maintained. Student enrollment, i.e., 23% more
                   students from individualized course selected
                   economics as their major than those from
                   traditional course.

                   *Done with control and experimental groups of
                   matched students.

12. James C. McKeown
    College of Commerce and Business Administration
    University of Illinois at Urbana-Champaign
    Urbana, Illinois

    Application: Computer Assisted Elementary Accounting

    Inputs: Computer programs for presenting instructional
                    materials and problems, generating unique sets of
                    data to be used in problems, and providing
                    individual diagnostic/remedial routines. In
                    addition, the programs are designed to record
                    student performance and control assignment of
                    materials and problems.

    Production: In conjunction with reading regular text materials,
                    students complete problems individually at
                    terminals. Computer responds to student answers
                    and presents subsequent data and questions in
                    appropriate sequence. Assistance in completing
                    problems is given through terminals with
                    introductory materials and diagnosic routines.
                    Additional explanatory materials and problems are
                    provided for students who need further help.
                    Instructors receive records of student performance
                    for follow-up.

    Outputs: Test results, i.e., students using computer
                    assisted accounting scored 9-10 points higher on
                    182-point final examination than did students
                    taking same course without computer assistance
                    (significant at .01 level). Student efficiency,
                    i.e., students using computer assistance completed
                    homework assignments in 10(24%) to 14(33%) hours
                    less than students without computer did. In
                    addition, computer-assisted students completed 19%
                    to 31% more homework problems than other students
                    within the above time periods.

                    Estimate per student contact hour cost $.62
                    (exclusive of development, maintenance, personnel,
                    or space costs).

13. Gerald G. Robine
    120 Special Education Building
    The Pennsylvania State University
    University Park, Pennsylvania

    Application: CAI Special Education Course

Inputs: Dedicated computer system including terminals and programs to provide questions/responses; to test achievement/performance; and to maintain and produce student records.

Production: Students follow diagnostic teaching models by interacting individually with terminals. They identify characteristics of children and select appropriate techniques, materials, and strategies for working with particular children. Computer responds immediately to each student and generates questions for his tests and examinations. Complete records of each student's performance in the course can be produced by the system.

Outputs: Test results, i.e., in comparative study of matched groups, students using computerized approach scored 24% higher on final examinations (criterion) than students who took conventional course (primarily lecture/discussion). This difference was statistically significant at .01 level. Student efficiency, i.e., students in same study who used computer assisted program completed course in 33% less time than those in conventional program. Per student computing costs for the course (exclusive of equipment) was $20 to $40, which compared favorably to standard tuition of $96 for the course (in-state students).

Additional
Reference: Cartwright, Carol A., Cartwright, G. Phillip, and Robine, Gerald G., "CAI Course in Early Identification of Handicapped Children," Exceptional Children, February, 1972.

14. John W. Wick
Chicago Board of Education
Chicago, Illinois

Application: Computerized Drill and Practice Reading

Inputs: Dedicated computer system including terminals and programs which provide exercises and feedback; maintain student records, and print reports. Special inservice training program and teaching assistants to help regular classroom teachers.

Production: Students work individually at computer terminals for 20 minutes each day. They complete diagnostic tests, drill and practice exercises based on those

tests, and mastery tests. Computer responds to
each student's answer, keeps track of his
performance, and controls presentation of
appropriate questions to him. Detailed reports of
each student's performance are given by computer to
individual students (their own only), classroom
teachers, and school administrators for evaluation
and follow-up.

Outputs:　Test scores, i.e., average student gain on
standardized achievement tests in reading of 1.1
years in eight months. Added costs for above
inputs were more than offset by this test gain,
because no other compensatory program for
disadvantaged children produced such results in
reading.

Additional
Reference:　Bone, Jan, "Turning on with CAI," American
Education, November, 1974.

15. Thomas H. Kent
Department of Pathology
College of Medicine
University of Iowa
Iowa City, Iowa

Application:　Computer Management
General and Systemic Pathology Courses for Medical
Students

Inputs:　A bank of multiple-choice test items developed and
shared by many institutions. Computer programs for
creating and managing the bank, for producing
Coursewriter III unit tests from the bank of
questions, for tracking and summarizing student
progress in the course, and for analyzing student
test results to produce test and item performance
statistics.

Production:　Faculty specifies course tests for the bank of
questions, and the items chosen are reformatted
into Coursewriter III unit tests. Students advance
on a self-paced basis through the course. They
order their tests by unit content area and the test
versions that cover the topic specified are
assigned randomly by the computer. At any time
during the course the supervisor may order a
summary of student progress. At the end of the
course, test and item performance statistics are

produced from a computerized analysis of student records.

Outputs: Faculty and staff efficiency: In the General and Systemic Pathology Course in 1974, 85 exams of predictable difficulty levels were prepared for student practice and course evaluation. Approximately 4,000 individual exams were administered during the 1974 academic year. Student satisfaction and efficiency: Students show a strong preference for self-paced course work; 95% favored self-pacing in the GP Course in 1974; 86% in the 1974 SP Course. On the average students completed the didactic units 3 1/2 weeks before the end of the course. There was no decline in student performance (and possibly some improvement).

THE UNIVERSITY AS VIDEOPUBLISHER OF LAST RESORT

C. B. Bowen
Cable Television and the University
Proceedings of the Conference
(January, 1974)

THE TRADITIONAL THINGS OF LEARNING

Education has been religious in purpose far longer than it has been secular, and that legacy is important in instructional procedure, and in instructional mediation. The monastery and the cloister gave us campus-based instruction, not the moveable feasts of itinerant scholars and their students (the medieval open university, if you please) but fixed instructional plant, high walls, trees, and residences for scholars and students. The tutorial emerged directly from catechism; indeed the magic classroom size (30) emerges from Talmudic instruction, as Alvin Eurich has stated.[2] As it was with the campus, and with the lecture, so it was with instructional things. The substance of learning was recorded by the prevailing labor-intensive technology, and the scribes devoted lifetimes first to accurately copying the text and later to embellishing the page.

Perhaps the immediate ancestors of university publishers were these scribes attached to monasteries, charged with the obligation to preserve the precious libraries of handwritten books by making meticulous handwritten copies, often adding decoration and embellishment. The copying of text was done with great care, exhaustively proofread (for errors might involve heresy), then given headings and title pages of suitable graphic grandeur, and, finally, bound. The glorious era of handwritten manuscripts and bound books was a massive step forward from previous devices for preserving thought and carrying it over distances in time and space; and the orderly procedures of proofreading and editorial care which were then followed continue to this day to preserve a text from one time and place to another.

The first textbooks — that is to say, those works studied or consulted in the process of instruction for whatever purpose — were copied books; they correspond to the modes of encoding then prevalent, but were not widely used. They were costly, cumbersome, perishable, and for all these reasons, access to them was highly restricted. It was the lawyers, who consulted text far more than the churchmen, who for reasons of convenience first changed the structure of written compilations from the roll to the book as we know it, with pages bound along one edge.

If the scribes were the scholarly publishers of their day, the antecedents of the publishers of textbooks may be found in the university students of former times who sought to provide their own low-priced copies of the classics. The historic role of the teacher in an early university was to read aloud from the classics at dictation speeds to gatherings of students. Rashdall, the great historian of medieval universities, suggests that the lecture then came to be divided into two parts: first, the reading of the text so that students could copy it, and second, selections of the most significant passeges within the text and commentary upon them. Later Odofredus, lecturing (the word dervies from the Latin, *legere*, to read) at Bologna in the early thirteenth century, augmented the dictated text as follows: "First, I shall give you summaries of each topic before I proceed to the text; secondly, I shall give you as clear and explicit a statement as I can of the purport of each Law; thirdly, I shall read the text with a view to correcting it; fourthly, I shall briefly repeat the contents of the Law and any distinctions or subtle and useful problems arising out of the Law with their solutions.[3]

Students, as enterprising then as now, quickly came to make arrangements with stationers who for a fee copied lecture transcriptions, or booksellers who rented out copies of full sets of transcriptions for the year. So much for the Italian line of descent for our textbook publishing. The other great university of that time, Paris, ". . . had its own statute on lecturing. Here the intention is to prevent the student from taking full notes — to prevent the publication and distribution of the masters' property. A later statute indicates the reaction of the students [to this early application of the principles of copyright]: 'scolars who throw stones at masters who speak too rapidly are to be fined.' "[4] The genealogy of textbook publishing thus had a proper combination of Italian enterpreneurship and French concern for proprietorship; it remains only to observe that so little changes with time.

As I have noted, education has been religious far longer than it has been secular. To the educational monopoly of the early Church, the monastic schools, that secular substance came first in the Norse sagas, the *Song of Roland,* and the *Nibelungenlied*; and finally into this cleft marched the whole of the classical past — Greek philosophy, Roman law. The medieval university, a scholastic institution embracing both the Christian and the classic past, was born. Its masters and students, bound by religious observation and practice, lived communally. It was poor, but portable; and although relatively free from constraining forces of the church, the state, or the local populace, such fragile institutions were given sanction by both pope and emperor, which meant that a degree from any one institution was acceptable throughout Western Europe. Teachers, students, and indeed, whole institutions, could move at will from place to place. The substance of the programs of these universities is of less concern to us than their teaching methodology, and, most pertinent, their use of instructional materials. For all faculties — theology, law, medicine, and philosophy —

> . . .The method was the same. In theology it consisted in acquiring the summa, the total body of the logical knowledge gradually worked out in the system of the theological doctors. In medicine, it was the learning of the medical body of knowledge laid down in the system of the Hippocratic-Galenic tradition. In jurisprudence, the student learned the body of the Roman and Church law. And in the philosophical faculty there was a regular body of Aristotelian and mathematical knowledge which was considered authoritative. In a word it was the textbook method. The books were meticulously

divided into puncta (periods?), and professors were fined at Bologna if they did not reach the proper points at the proper time.[5]

Thus, working through a subject, relieved regularly by discussion, and after rigorous examination (the baccalaureate examination at Paris lasted some televe hours, through which the candidate remained standing), a student moved to his successive degrees. Specialities developed; one went to Salerno for medicine, Bologna for law, Paris for theology. But the full flowering of instructional use of the conserved word awaited the invention, or at least the application, of the new technology of movable type.

An historical view of the evolution of the textbook illumines the universe of other instructional things. From the beginning, the textbook offered substance, that body of learning was to be conveyed across time and space from mentor to student. But it also came to offer a structure, the instructional strategy of presentation. The textbook was, and is, a highly ordered learning instrument; it presumes a curriculum and conserves its subjects' place therein. It creates a lesson plan or syllabus to guide both teacher and student. It offers interaction, through questions and answers, study or research assignments, suggestions for further reading and integration of further reading with the text. And increasingly it came to offer evaluation, self-administered examinations to quizzes, to help the student find his way through the lesson. If the elements sound familiar — substance, structure, strategy, performance measures — it is because the textbook from mid-nineteenth century America to much of the world today constitutes not merely the foremost, but the solitary instructional "thing" used by most teachers. Teachers have been trained to use textbooks; they enjoy the freedom to chose or select among many optional texts; they may adapt their course work from greater to lesser conformity with the substance and arrangement of a given text; and, critically, they hold the prospect of creating their own text if none exists to serve the course as they wish to teach it.

Contrast this with the circumstance facing visual (read video) courseware or textbooks: Teachers are not trained to use non-print instructional stuff. There is little organized distribution and supply of non-print material. An instructor is constrained to use the non-print material as given, if at all, and further constrained in time, place, physical circumstance, and other logistical concerns. Further, if no such material exists for his course, he is constrained by skills and cost from creating his own; it is as though each instructor who wished to write a textbook were obliged to take his ideas to the bazaar and hire a scribe to set down the text, and then never see mass reproduction of the copy, but rather other handwritten copies.

Thus, the elements which have defeated instructional television and frustrated the full visual and textual presentation of subject matter, whatever the field of study, are still with us. We have infinitely increased the speed and flexibility of text copying; from moveable type, the invention of the typewriter, the production of mass market editions of texts, and the growth of better copying devices, text and graphic presentation of subject matter have been vastly enhanced. The constraints upon the non-print media, constraints of entrepreneurship, proprietorship, originating or authoring competence, mechanisms for inexpensive reproduction, widespread distribution, and resulting economics of scale resulting in lower cost — all these still constrain lie the non-print media.

116

REFERENCES

.   Eurich, Alan C.: oral communication
3.   Rashdall, Hastings: The Universities of Europe in the Middle
      Ages; Oxford, 1936, Vol. I, p. 218
4.   Fehl, Noah E.: The Idea of a University in East and West Hong
      Kong; Chung Che College, 1962; p. 188
5.   Mueller, Gustav E., Education Limited; Norman: University of
      Oklahoma Press, 1949, p. 129

APPLICATIONS

Computers

A second chance for computer-aided instruction

What networking promised but didn't deliver may be developed at the local level as hardware costs drop

The lure of computer-aided instruction (CAI) is once again being felt by those who have maintained their interest in this problem-ridden educational tool and believe that advances in the technology will give it another chance. In the late 1960s, it was supposedly going to revolutionize the learning process; the best teachers were going to write "courseware" (interactive educational computer programs) that would be nationally distributed. Students would learn rapidly and efficiently. However, reality turned out to be quite different from the dream—so far.

A few people did take the time to study the medium's potential, and did produce outstanding computer educational material. But CAI development, which has remained in the hands of a relatively small community of experts, has yet to develop as much courseware as had been predicted. Except for grade-school drill and practice, it also has yet to overcome the general reluctance of the educational community to adopt it on a wide scale.

Consider Plato, for example—Program Logic for Automated Teaching Operations. It is by far the largest general-purpose CAI installation. (Plato development centers, as well as other major CAI sites, are listed in Table I.) Plato is both an interactive network for delivering CAI, and, via its programming language (Tutor, which is derived from Fortran), a means of lesson writing.

According to its originator, Donald Bitzer, some 16 000 hours of CAI-related material have been created for Plato, of which about 4000 hours are used regularly for CAI. But those 16 000 hours represent a total of 500–800 thousand hours of writing. And where do the "good" 4000 hours go? They are used primarily at Plato's original site at the University of Illinois. The university also services 185 additional sites, though in those areas terminals tend to be few and far between with a total of 1100 terminals in the system—an average of less than ten per site. Half of the Illinois program material (2000 hours) is distributed by the Control Data Corporation (CDC), which maintains a Plato time-share network and also tries to sell complete systems to other users.

The only other complete Plato system in active use is at the University of Delaware, where two thirds of the terminals and computers are now being used just to develop new material. Another alternative, time-shared CDC Plato at $1130 per month per terminal for unlimited use, has been used for commercial training programs but has had few subscribers in a school system, according to CDC.

Even with this demonstrated market resistance, Dr.

Bitzer foresees a nationwide network of as many as a million CAI terminals. At the rate of 50 hours of writing per hour of courseware for an experienced author, excluding support services, that represents a lot of work—especially when, by Dr. Bitzer's estimation, the amount of courseware increases exponentially with the number of terminals.

Establishing CAI goals

Many feel that the solution to future CAI growth is not simply financing an army of CAI authors. A better way, the say, would be to find the areas in which CAI is most effective, and then devise some effective tool for creating and testing good courseware addressed to those areas. This more or less was the substance of a March 1978 report, "Computers and the Learning Society," prepared by the Subcommittee on Domestic and International Planning of the House Committee on Science and Technology.

Such courseware goals are not made easier by the diversity of CAI components and educational models. Among the elements in a sample CAI program may be dialogue, problem solving, simulation, drill and practice, exploration, quizzes—indeed, all the components that go into classroom learning processes. Even the same mix of material may be presented in totally different ways, depending on the educational philosophy of the authors.

So far, testing for CAI efficacy has not shown that CAI for general education is superior to any other means of teaching, except for drill and practice. But even if CAI were found to be merely a cost-effective educational supplement and superior to humans only under certain well-defined conditions, these limitations might not hinder its future acceptance if they were clearly stated.

The problem with evaluating Plato courseware as a whole, in this context, is not its quality. It is that Tutor, the Plato course-generating language, was deliberately designed to be used without any underlying instructional strategy being built in; in that way, every author could provide his or her own pedagogical features. The strategy worked well in that a reasonable amount of material was—and still is—generated by many different authors. Of course, approval for Plato was thus built up among the authoring peer group. However, the strategy may have backfired in the sense that overall Plato program evaluation is difficult because there are no unifying objectives. Many authors may thus be tempted to "reinvent" the wheel by reexecuting lessons that are already in the catalogue.

Assuming that CAI proves worthwhile in some well-defined sense, there still remains the problem of convincing skeptics in the academic establishment to give it a try,

---

Robert Sugarman   Associate Editor

IEEE spectrum AUGUST 1978

especially at a time when schools are facing declining student populations. The problem is the usual slowness of change of any complex sociological system, particularly that of education. As CAI researcher Alfred Bork (of the University of California at Irvine) points out, 200 years passed after the invention of the printing press before books began to be widely used.

Various scenarios have been concocted by CAI enthusiasts about when and how its acceptance will come about, but all agree it is too early to predict which model, if any, will predominate (see box on page 35).

Decreasing hardware cost

Inextricably mixed with the future of CAI is the anticipated decrease in the cost of its hardware-delivery systems. This is true of computing in general but especially of CAI, which up to now has had to be implemented on comparatively expensive time-share systems (see Table I) costing half a million dollars or more. The switch to potentially cheaper distributed computing, where much of the program interaction takes place locally on "standalone" intelligent terminals, should make more institutions willing to make a commitment to CAI.

The standalone transition, however, may not be immediate because adopting central-computer programs to remote use is not a trivial task. Even Dr. Bitzer, the major proponent of time-shared CAI, admits the transition is technically feasible, but he argues that central time sharing will not die out because of the variety of additional interactive educational services it can offer. However, the cost savings to be had by putting most of the intelligence required for student–program interaction in a local terminal instead of a central computer is so great that it may eventually replace time-shared CAI entirely.

For example, Florida State University estimates the cost for a 45-terminal time-share system, excluding courseware royalty costs, to be some $3 an hour per terminal locally, going to $4 some 300 miles away. Beyond this limit, one must figure telephone costs at about one dollar per mile per hour for an eight-user link. In contrast to this, a $5000–$6000 standalone system at today's prices amortizes to 50 cents to a dollar per system hour, assuming normal 1500-hour/year usage and excluding maintenance.

The price figure mentioned for a standalone system is in the range quoted for a standalone floppy-disk loaded intelligent cathode-ray-tube station made for educational use by Terak of Scottsdale, Ariz. It is also within the range predicted for a conceptually similar terminal being readied for Plato standalone use by Dr. Bitzer's group. Other manufacturers, including Digital, Wang, and Hewlett-Packard, offer similar equipment, although it is probably not as precisely tailored to CAI's needs.

Typical of the relative savings to be had in switching from time-share to standalone, Professor Bork estimates that it now costs $75 per student semester to operate a Honeywell Sigma 7 on time-share in a physics course that makes extensive use of CAI. He says that cost could drop to $25 by switching to the Terak.

But neither Dr. Bork nor Dr. Bitzer sees total standalone operation as desirable since there must remain some method of student–faculty communication (electronic mail), answering immediate calls for help, generating and filing quizzes, and storing student progress. Dr. Bork is designing a central mini- or microcomputer with about 20 megabytes of disk storage for this purpose. A student sitting at a standalone station who wanted to take a quiz in a particular course would first query the central computer to see if he or she were eligible, and if eligible would receive the test from the central computer.

The Delaware Plato group plans to convert from time-share Plato to Dr. Bitzer's standalone intelligent terminal within five years. But authoring on Plato, which requires a lot more computer resources than does student interaction, would still continue to take place on their central computers.

Costs are expected to decrease with time for both time-share and "mostly" standalone systems, such as those that would use Dr. Bitzer's intelligent terminal. While many people believe that standalone will remain the cheaper of the two, Dr. Bitzer himself continues to feel that standalone will only be justified for terminals geographically remote from a central computer. It is true that if some of the experiments CDC is now performing with intelligent network switching come to fruition, the cost of long-distance Plato time-share might be cut by a factor of four to eight. CDC envisions a network of intelligent microprocessor-driven multiplexers that assign Plato data bandwidths on a usage basis, the key being that present terminals fixed at a 1200-baud rate only need an average of one fourth to one eighth of that speed.

But such a net also makes standalone Plato more attractive, since a standalone terminal only occasionally accessing the central computer would generally require less bandwidth; at present it must be assigned the full 1200-baud channel. On the other hand, if CDC develops enough geographically clustered potential customers to justify sideband CATV transmission of Plato material, which does not interact with main-channel broadcasting, transmission costs would drop even more for time-shared Plato. The needed return-line bandwidth from the Plato terminal to the computer is so small, since the user hits only a very few keys a second, that return telephone costs would be comparatively trivial.

Looking at time-share versus standalone cost from another aspect, it is true that the cost of electronic intelligence at the chip level is coming down as fast for large central computers as for microcomputers. But the hardware cost of packaging this intelligence is likely to be far less because of the economics of volume production at the user end where as many as 1000 standalone computers would be used as opposed to a single mainframe for time-share.

While "standalone" may be CAI's wave of the future, it is also not entirely clear whether even the present and proposed Terak and Plato "mostly" standalone systems are adequate for all CAI lessons. The microcomputer used in the Terak, a Digital LSI-11, which has a 16-bit word length and an extra floating-point hardware chip, may be fast enough to handle some of the rather intricate graphical calculations currently done via a time-sharing system, Dr. Bork says.

Dr. Bitzer feels that the 8-bit 8080 microprocessor used in time-share Plato terminals for miscellaneous chores is fast enough for some—but not all—Plato standalone calculations. In particular, he feels that a "parser" routine, which makes sense of student questions even if they have the wrong syntax or are misspelled, might require the next generation microprocessor following the 8080. This is Intel's 16-bit 8086, which is reported to have about ten times the 8080's speed.

Another problem with standalone systems of the future

is going to be the size of their random-access memory (RAM). Theoretically, a terminal needs only a relatively small RAM workspace, provided a floppy disk can load "overlays" of memory into RAM as needed, and provided time is not wasted transferring data back and forth from the RAM to the disk.

Dr. Bork feels this transfer-time loss will not be a problem for him on the Terak, but Dr. Bitzer and his group, with a somewhat different design goal, are not certain they would be able to avoid problems. Their intent in creating a "standalone" Plato is to build into each terminal an abridged version of the Tutor interpreter now residing in Plato central-computer storage. This so-called micro-Tutor will translate Tutor commands on the disk into microprocessor language. But to save fast-access memory space and money, they are trying to compress the interpreter into some 16k bytes of fast permanent read-only memory (ROM). This may not be enough, they report, to include the "parser."

The local memory problem is far more complex for some of the courses in logic developed by Patrick Suppes

[1] Unlike most computer programming, the human and machine links that form a CAI system are complex, and vary greatly from one authoring system to another. For standalone student use the program is transcribed in student-loaded floppy disks. If student progress records are to be kept, a central computer is necessary whether or not the student has a standalone terminal. The teacher communicates with the record file via the teacher display. When the student calls for help beyond what the program can provide and the teacher is not in the same room, teacher and student communicate via their terminals.

and his Stanford University coworkers, who may make use of several hundred thousand words of central-computer storage to check students' mathematical proofs. It would be a formidable task to transpose these to floppy-disk data overlays and the group does not have any plans for doing so.

Another problem faced by authoring groups, such as those of Drs. Bork and Suppes, that give courses with a large CAI component is that the material for a single course may require several disks. Dr. Bork is willing to go to multiple floppy drives or a floppy library to overcome this problem, but Dr. Suppes feels that a student should be given instant and easy access to all the material in a course if desired for review purposes.

Needed hardware

Many CAI systems, such as Plato and Stanford University's, already have continuous-speech peripherals based on computer assembly of a spoken dictionary or of basic phonemes. Plato also has program-assigned and labeled touch inputs in any of 256 screen locations. Terak is planning on a graphic digitizer of finer resolution. The graphic screen grid of 512 by 512 elements as used by Plato is certainly adequate, all agree, for any but the most specialized of today's CAI programs. Terak's grid, 340 by 220, may also be adequate, but Terak will improve it in subsequent models.

What is lacking is color and shading for graphic images. Such images can also benefit from some form of standalone source of graphic storage, which would allow a

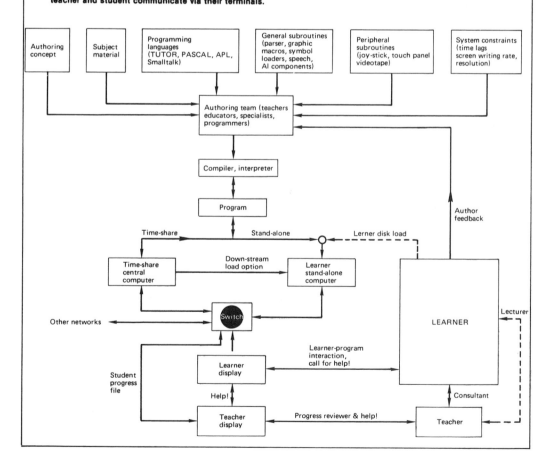

great deal of CAI graphics to be put into still frames or video sequences, without resorting to computer generation. Random-access video-disk players that can provide storage are on the market, but at $5000 are still too expensive for general use. (Where the intent of the CAI complement is to have a student alter the image, a video disk cannot be used.)

Another hardware improvement that could profoundly affect CAI programming would be a speed increase for today's standalone computers from, say, several hundred thousand instruction per second to 100 million. Alan Kay of the Xerox Park Learning Research Group (LRG) says this change would finally free the user from the tyranny of the programmer at all system levels. At this speed, he feels, real-time systems could be written in some easily learnable user language without having to worry about execution rates. Musical synthesis could, for example, be written by a musician for any musical instrument or by a cartoonist for high-speed animation. Even at six million instructions per second (MIPS)—the speed of the present Xerox experimental personal computers—this must still

[2] Two frames from a chemistry simulation program, by Stan Smith of Plato-Illinois, designed to save broken glassware and wasted distillation fractions before the students actually perform the experiment.

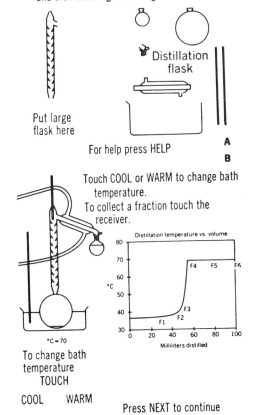

Here are the parts to a distillation apparatus. Put the apparatus together by touching a piece and then touching where it goes on the column.

Distillation flask

Put large flask here

For help press HELP

A
B

Touch COOL or WARM to change bath temperature.
To collect a fraction touch the receiver.

Distillation temperature vs. volume

°C = 70

To change bath temperature
TOUCH

COOL   WARM

Press NEXT to continue

be done in microcode, which, Mr. Kay feels, "no one but a computer hacker would wish to write."

Going from 6 to 100 MIPS within the next decade theoretically can be achieved by stringing together a number of microprocessors—provided the formidable architectural problem of linking them effectively can be solved.

Present and future courseware

Unlike hardware, courseware is not likely to improve in the immediate future.

Various authoring systems do exist where success seems inversely proportional to the generality of their goals. For example, Patrick Suppes' two groups, at Stanford and at the Computer Curriculum Corporation (CCC), seem to be mastering two specialized but highly nontrivial areas: grade-school drill and practice, and teaching university mathematics courses entirely by computer.

For the former, he has created an elaborate statistical model, proprietary to CCC, that analyzes student performance in order to choose drill and practice that has the right degree of difficulty. Under a grant from the National Institute of Education, the Princeton-based Educational Testing Service (ETS) is currently evaluating this work; but data from other sources seem to indicate that CAI drill and practice is generally effective.

For the introductory Stanford logic courses, Dr. Suppes' group has constructed English-to-logic and logic-to-English parsers and artificial intelligence logic-proof checkers, but is still working on variants of the proof checkers and on educational models to determine when a student has sufficient mastery of a lesson to go on to the next one.

At the other end of the generality spectrum, Plato leaves goals and learning techniques entirely up to each author. Although it has been used as the major content of a course more often than it has been used for separate lessons, each classroom teacher can select the material he or she deems most appropriate.

Because the CAI information and communication links between author, student, classroom teacher, and the computer are so complex, and because there are so many different stratagems for authoring, it may be helpful here to discuss other CAI learning approaches.

At the point indicated by the "Learner" box in Fig. 1, the learner interacts with the computer and requests help—when needed—from the program, or from a local or remote teacher. The student ought also to be able to enter comments on the quality of the material. Some authoring systems, including Ticcit, described below, claim they can preguess student problems with the material; others, including Dr. Bork and the Plato authors, depend partially on student feedback.

Stan Smith, considered one of Plato's most gifted author/programmers, says this feedback is essential for success. "A major difference between CAI and a textbook," he explains, "is that I can, in theory—but hopefully not in practice—bring out a new courseware edition every evening, based on student feedback of the day's classes."

The teacher in CAI occupies a position that seems to vary with each authoring concept. In Plato, the teacher continues as lecturer since the system, in most cases, is used for lessons, rather than for a complete course. But in many CAI courses the teacher no longer lectures but acts as a consultant and helper to the student. When the

[3] Alfred Bork's discovery programs require sophisticated computer-user interaction to lead to self-discovery of the laws of physics—in this case, the location and polarity of electrical charges.

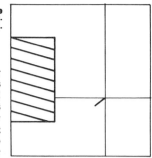

Back to our covered charges.
Point anywhere you'd like to begin.
Here is your electric field vector at that point.
This vector establishes a direction at that point characteristic of the field.

course or lessons have a high exam content, the teacher may act in the conventional way as a selector of quizzes and remedial material, but in many cases the CAI operating system makes the selection. The teacher serves as an adviser to individual students, and dealing with their problems on a one-to-one basis, rather than acting primarily as an authority figure, is hardly threatening to university professors, who may relegate part of their teaching to graduate students, and who may even have authored programs. However, status change is reported by many, including CDC, to be threatening to grade-school teachers.

After the author or authoring team has decided on the role of the teacher, a substantial and complex set of resources is drawn upon to create a program. The team must also take into account the peripherals to be used in the system, perhaps even doing things like programming both with and without voice articulation because they do not know which users have access to that peripheral.

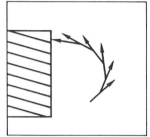

Point to another place a small distance from the first point in this direction.

The new vector sets a slightly different direction. Step ahead a small distance in this new direction.

Having decided on some pedagogical concept, and the various physical restraints of the system, the authors must decide on a programming language. In addition to Tutor, other typical languages are Pascal and APL, Fortran and Lisp.

Who does the programming? There are at least two distinct procedures. The classical route, most often but not always taken by Plato, is the one where the authors are programmers. Elsewhere—Dr. Bork's group, for example—a team of two faculty members outlines flow charts for the material, which is coded by student programmers. In Dr. Suppes' group, there is a similar process, with graduate student programmers also selecting the difficulty of some of the lesson examples.

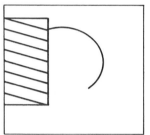

Let's continue the process.
This picture is a mess!
Let's simplify it, getting rid of the arrows and showing only the direction.
At a given point on this line, the electric field vector is
_____ to this new line.

Authoring concepts

Authoring concepts seem to fall into three main categories. In the first, used by Plato, the general direction of student responses tends to be preguessed by the authors. The learner gets to make right or wrong answers but has little choice in the level of difficulty of the material.

Good Plato courseware, however, transcends any simplistic definition. Figure 2 shows two "frames" of a simulation lesson by Stan Smith, in which the student, using mainly the screen-touch panel, first assembles glassware for a distillation and then runs the distillation at a student-controlled time-varying temperature. The computer analyzes the purity of each distillation phase and helps the student to select which samples will be submitted to it as being of the desired purity. In creating this program, Dr. Smith has used so many authoring tricks to involve the student in the program that it is sometimes difficult for people who are viewing it for the first time to keep in mind that the rather simple graphical images are only a simulation.

Another authoring approach is to define the teaching system as discovery-oriented. Dr. Bork, for example, has created a number of graphic programs in the physical sciences that use a complex interaction of computer and student to simulate the real world (with the computer-aided addition of visible field lines) so that the student can

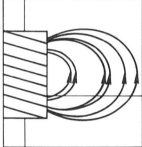

We could also follow it in the opposite direction.
We'll put an arrowhead on the line to indicate the direction of the field.
I'll draw a few more field lines for you. Just point!
Would you like to draw some more field lines? No

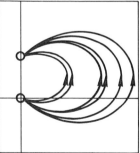

By now you may have some idea about where the charges are located!
Do you? Sure
Point to the location of the charges.

Let's remove the cover and show both the charges and the field lines.
Do the two charges have the same sign?
Please answer yes or no!
No
I agree.
Point to the positive charge.

discover some of the basic rules of physics. Figure 3 shows a few frames from such a dialogue, wherein the student asks the computer to draw field lines in (student)-selected areas. The goal is for the student to discover the nature and location of the electric charges producing those lines, and thus build up insight into the manner in which such systems behave.

Such discovery programs could be published much like a textbook with a quiz component added by individual classroom instructors. Dr. Bork is working both in computer management of quizzes and with these discovery programs, and says both are essential ingredients of a full CAI course. In any event, until graphic CAI computer usage becomes more universal, there exists no nationwide hardware-delivery system for such a textbook.

Another approach is for the authors to help the student to become an excellent learning strategist, at a minimum of two levels of strategy. At the lowest level, the student chooses the difficulty of the rule, example, and practice combinations involved. A special auxiliary keyboard (Fig. 4) is used to let the student select the difficulty of each of those for the next frame. Ticcit, which stands for Time-Shared Interactive Computer-Controlled Information Television, is such an approach. As originally conceived by the Mitre Corporation and implemented by Victor Bunderson and John Volk, it uses Sony color television as a display of both computer-generated text and video-taped graphic images.

Testing Plato and Ticcit

Both Plato and Ticcit were tested during 1975 and 1976 by ETS for the National Science Foundation (NSF) at a community-college level in basic mathematics and English. Unlike Plato, the Ticcit teacher acted as an aide, not a lecturer. The results were mixed.

For Ticcit, ETS found that CAI courses had a markedly lower completion rate than comparable teacher-led courses, especially where students had low pretest scores. On the other hand, students who did finish Ticcit courses had, on the average, 5 percent higher test scores on final exams than students in teacher-taught courses. Another problem was that students in the Ticcit project felt ignored as individuals, compared with students in teacher-led courses. Conversely, ETS found that students' grades were little affected one way or another by using Plato, and that most students enjoyed the medium.

Ticcit's high dropout rate, the ETS evaluators comment, is not unknown in other self-paced learning environments where those who feel unable to control their environment, or don't wish to compete, drop behind or out. From 1975 to 1977, Victor Bunderson and his colleagues at Brigham Young University investigated the ef-

I. Some of the major computer-aided instructional development centers (all graphic terminals except there noted)

Group and Principal Investigators	Central Computer	Communications Net	Terminal	CAI Component
Plato-Illinois, Donald Bitzer, computer-based Education Research Laboratory	Four interlinked processors (CDC6500 and Cyber 73) Two million words of core, one million solid state	Local microwave; remote by phone to 185 sites including 42 colleges	1100 terminals mostly Plato IV, some Plato V	350 local terminals at Illinois for 71 general subjects, most courses in physics, chemistry, foreign language, medicine, and accounting
CDC time-share Plato	CDC central-computer base	130 cities in U.S. with dedicated 9600-baud lines, eight users to a line	Plato V	Illinois plus CDC courseware; commercial training; CAI integrated with mastery exams
Plato, University of Delaware, Fred Hofstetter	Cyber 73, 500k-word memory	Telephone	75 Plato V	General
Plato, Florida State	Cyber 73 and 74, 500k-word memory	Telephone	45 Plato IV	General
Ticcit, Victor Bunderson and John Volk	Nova 800 terminal processor Nova 840 main processor	Local or remote	Sony color TV sets, 30 at Brigham Young University, 128 each at two junior colleges, 128 at Model Secondary School for the Deaf	English and mathematics
Patrick Suppes, Computer Curriculum Corp.	Nova 800 minicomputer	Local time-share	4000 to 5000 alphanumeric terminals, each 80 characters by 24 lines	CMI drill and practice grades K through 6, English and math
Stanford University, Patrick Suppes, Institute for Mathematical Studies in the Social Sciences	DEC KI 10 with 512k-word memory and Miss audio synthesizer	Local time-share	50 alphanumeric terminals, each 80 characters by 24 lines	Four complete math courses, several partial language courses, computer speech generation
University of California at Irvine, Alfred Bork Educational Technology Center	Sigma 7; DEC system 20	Local time-share	45 type 4013 Tektronix storage tube, 14 Terak	Complete courses in physics, mathematics, anthropology
University of California at San Diego, Kenneth Bowles	None	None	20-Terak stand-alone terminals	Courses in Pascal; automated quizzes following Alfred Bork's CMI work

IEEE spectrum AUGUST 1978

fect of social variables, such as the formation of small groups, on completion rates. They reported completion rates of more than 90 percent.

In spite of the finding of no significant impact on student achievement, 80 to 83 percent of the instructors judged Plato to have a positive effect on such achievement. Whether this effect was real but not measurable, or only subjective, was not evaluated by ETS.

Ticcit could not be tested elsewhere at the time since only three courses had been developed. Plato was, and is, used elsewhere, of course, with particularly good results being reported for fourth-grade mathematics. However, ETS did not go beyond the community-college level in testing Plato.

There are no longer any immediate plans to expand Ticcit for general education, although replacement of the video tape by a video disk, which would give the system standalone capability, may change the picture. Courseware, Inc., a San Diego-based company, has had success, however, in writing Ticcit-like material in both CAI and printed formats for the military, and is in fact under contract to CDC to write a Ticcit-based training course for Plato. The Courseware designers report that although Ticcit authoring concepts are difficult, once mastered they enable speedy production of high-quality, goal-oriented material.

System Development Goal

Develop standalone Plato V terminal; 9600-baud multiplexing in 1978; explore communication net expansion with CDC

Intelligent message switching network to allow 32 users per line; side-channel CATV transmission

Double system size and number of terminals in 1978; switchover within five years to standalone Plato V

Conversion to up-to-date CDC Plato operating system

Ticcit licensee Hazeltine has two military training systems, expects additional installations

Color, graphics by early 1980s

Improved speech generation, more sophisticated artificial intelligence proof checkers to determine lesson mastery

Phased switchover to Terak standalone, using Pascal from University of California, San Diego

Making Pascal software transportable to a variety of microprocessor systems

---

Sugarman—A second chance for computer-aided instruction

WICAI, Inc., a nonprofit company based in Orem, Utah, and headed by Victor Bunderson, has implemented a Ticcit-like learning strategy on a biology-based video disk for McGraw-Hill. The company is also developing material for standalone microprocessors that will incorporate lessons and learning strategies learned from the Ticcit project.

For the future

According to NSF, most important to CAI's future are explorations aimed not at achieving specific learning goals but at learning about learning through interactive computer use. The work of Alan Kay and Adele Goldberg and their associates at LRG is relevant here even though the group has nothing whatever to do with CAI since it avoids any "canned" material. Instead, it explores the way both children and adults can use the computer as an intelligent tool and as a learning resource.

Figure 5 shows the results of some of the programs written in a language called Smalltalk at LRG. The "team" consisted of a 13-year-old teacher supervising 12-year-old authors with only the basic tools for drawing precoded by LRG. Teams of the same age at LRG have developed far more complex systems, but the point is illustrated here that, given the right tools, a lot of authors ought to be able to write interesting programs—certainly for themselves, and possibly for others.

Overcoming obstacles

Thus far we have been discussing only those all-purpose CAI systems that seek to replace almost all the functions of the classroom teacher—either via programming goals (such as those of Drs. Suppes, Bork, and Bunderson), or by virtue of complex hardware (Plato, Ticcit). Such systems are certainly laudable; in theory only a computer has enough speed to respond instantly and individually to each separate learner in a classroom. Moreover, the computer can do so continually and simultaneously, providing each one with advice, illustrations, questions, feedback, and progress reports.

But since learning is still in its infancy as a cognitive science, with or without computers, it is not surprising that mainline CAI has made comparatively small progress in effectively providing one-on-one interactions. Realizing that the technique is still experimental, many educators have responded by using CAI as a complement to regular course offerings and adopting only the portions that are most cost effective.

This limited acceptance and use makes the necessary hardware and courseware both a lot simpler and cheaper. For example, there is no need for a back-up computer, or a terminal for the teacher, if CAI is going to be used only for simulation. That also simplifies the links between the teacher, learner, and author, since no attempt is being made to do more than carry on a rudimentary form of Socratic dialogue—in which the student presses one or two buttons, or uses the computer as a simple calculator.

In fact, home computers costing under $1000 are being used at the college level for just such purposes—for instance, Commodore's PET model microcomputer. At a cost of around $900 it offers not only alphanumeric text, but an extensive—though fixed—collection of graphic symbols that can be manipulated to form, for example, images of physical and chemical laboratory apparatus. (The use of such small systems in the classroom will be explored in a forthcoming issue of *Spectrum*.)

Primarily, however, where CAI is used in the elementary school classroom it is in addition to regular courses and human instructions, not as a complete substitute. The Computer Curriculum Corporation (see Table I) has, in the field, several thousand minicomputer-controlled terminals whose only purpose is to provide drill and practice.

There are communities that take an entirely different approach to CAI. Sylvia Charp, director of instructional systems for Philadelphia schools, says that 70 000 students, out of the 200 000 in the district, are involved in CAI programs administered on some 350 terminals tied to Hewlett-Packard minicomputers. Using either CRTs or teletypewriters—which she prefers because they give a hard-copy record—students get remedial drill and practice, simulation in courses like economics, and even job-counseling, all at a price of less than a dollar per terminal hour. Computer-managed quizzes cost from about 8 to 40 cents per hour, since the terminals are not connected to a complex hierarchical computer net.

Even a system like Plato might be cost-effective for applications where the terminal population is clustered locally, making telephone costs relatively inexpensive. Dr. Charp estimates that to substitute for the Philadelphia system might only cost two or three times more per hour on a time-shared basis.

The Chicago school system services about 15 000 educationally disadvantaged children in grade schools that have some 930 CRT displays using a single time-shared Univac main computer and software originally licensed from the CCC. Spending some ten minutes a day with the terminals in drill and practice is estimated to be the equivalent of about 60 minutes of work with a teacher.

A typical mix of CAI and non CAI programs can be found in Minnesota, where 800 000 students are instructed via 2000 terminals with low-speed time sharing from CDC and HP central computers. The average cost is around a dollar an hour, since the state picks up the additional cost of phone-connect time.

About 500 programs are offered, of which perhaps ten percent are CAI, including state-developed drill and practice. Plato is also offered, but there are only about 25 users, at 20 sites. CDC has offered to provide Plato time-share facilities to rural schools for about two dollars an hour. The company has not made clear whether that price includes courseware and/or telephone costs.

One widespread criticism among CAI users is that the programs need to become truly interactive, and ought to have more depth than any of today's material. One way to provide that depth is to put artificial intelligence (AI) into programs, so that the machine can not only decide whether a student's response is right or wrong, but if it is wrong can analyze why and respond in an appropriate manner. The student is thus allowed to experiment with and debug his or her own learning strategies.

Such programs will take a lot more memory to store and speed to execute than anything available in today's CAI systems. Yet present systems can be remarkably sophisticated. Dr. Suppes' group at Stanford University uses several hundred thousand words of PDP-10 storage for intelligence proof checkers, but still is not able to understand the students' learning strategies interactively. While waiting for the development of sufficient speed and

[4] A Ticcit auxiliary keyboard is used to select the level of difficulty of rules, practice, or examples to be shown in the next frame.

ATTN	EXIT	NOTE
GO	SKIP	BACK
OBJ	MAP	ADVICE
HELP	HARDER	EASIER
RULE	EXAMP	PRACT

```
ann      shape 5!
ann grow your size     50!
ann grow your size    —40!
ann grow your sides     3!
```

[5] Susan (top), Kathy (middle), and Dennis (bottom) at the Xerox LRG try their hand at writing programs in Smalltalk. They had to understand such procedures as dividing by negative numbers, testing inequalities, and counting with increments to create their lessons. Susan was interested in sending nine polygon messages to grow, turn, and copy itself and Kathy, in simulating rocketship travel. Dennis came up with a variety of operators and rocketship classes for war games.

CAI proliferation scenarios

Advocates of computer-aided instruction may give one or more of the following scenarios for its proliferation:

● Sudden miracle: This assumes the academic community will suddenly invest large sums of money in CAI research and in CAI delivery systems, based on a realization of CAI's intrinsic merit. This might occur for drill and practice at the grade-school level, but is most unlikely for university courses and for research because academic research, impossible without Government aid, needs Federal CAI funding. Such aid, which has amounted to some $232 million since 1965, is now down to a trickle of about $3 million per year.

● Osmotic, type A: This arguments says that the decreasing price of computer power will finally place so much of it within the school system for administration, grading, record keeping, and conventional classroom R&D projects that CAI will finally come into its own, if only as a means of fully amortizing all that computer power. This scenario makes sense for the future, since even as far back as 1974 higher education had spent some $650 million for computers, and secondary schools had spent $350 million for computer services. It also makes sense historically because many of the CAI installations shown in Table I are already comingled with other applications. Standalone CAI, with a low entry-level price is bound to help this scenario.

● Osmotic, type B: This scenario assumes that so much computer power will be in the hands of consumers—in the form of home computers and specialized learning devices like calculators and electronic spelling aids—that the schools will yield to consumer pressure and install their own competing devices.

● Private sector to the rescue: Here the computer manufacturers, who up to now have considered the educational market a stepchild, will make an about-face and supply the needed courseware and hardware. Control Data Corporation is already doing just that, but Texas Instruments, which has the financial and technical resources, is so far sticking to consumer educational devices. Learning Research Group (LRG), deep into theoretical concepts, denies any attempt to go commercial with its research.

On the other hand, it is not wise to underestimate the ingenuity of the private sector in harnessing mass production to perceived consumer needs, whether in the home or in the school. Texas Instruments has used a recorded speech vocabulary combined with linear predictive coding to produce a children's spelling aid that selects words from a ROM library, speaks, and checks spelling, which is keyboard entered and displayed, for correctness. The whole instrument, which has a microprocessor driving a time-variable digital filter, ROM library, keyboard, and alphanumeric starburst display, sells for $50.

Technology watchers report that companies like TI and Hewlett-Packard are capable of bringing out a home computer—this year, if they wish—that uses their own 16-bit microprocessors and is capable of providing "Saturday morning cartoon" graphics—i.e., animation—by moving a variety of ROM stored fixed images, much as in present TV games. Such animation, as opposed to computer-generated figures, would probably suffice for most of Plato courseware, but would not be adequate to implement Dr. Bork's work, or the Xerox LRG. The problem in marketing such a machine is whether enough images can be placed in memory at today's memory prices to make the machine cost effective.

● Government to the rescue. This course theoretically solves all the problems except one: who gets the money for what. It also assumes that Congress is willing to give up other educational priorities, which in the past it has refused to do. One possibility is funding of a national communication network costing $50 million and up. That might give new hope to supporters of a CAI computer network. Another is the formation of a national open university like that of England—but computerized, so that correspondence courses are mostly conducted by standalone terminals in the home. Cost for the courseware is estimated at some $300 million.

The NSF oversight committee might more realistically come out in favor of funding grade-school drill and practice, or setting up national test sites for CAI courseware evaluation. More modestly, the NSF, which has yet to receive any such grandiose funding, is continuing to dole out what few funds it has to researchers who are exploring the basic concepts of CAI as a cognitive tool, as opposed to just pounding out courseware.

As a footnote to the effectiveness of Government funding, it is worth noting that Control Data's Plato could never have made it without NSF funding.

memory in a commercially viable system, AI practitioners have already begun to develop the necessary learning algorithms. (More on these developments will follow in a forthcoming article on computer-aided instruction.)

The outlook

In summary, probably none of the present authoring concepts are immediately acceptable as the total solution to CAI's courseware problem—not because any have been proved inadequate but only because they have not yet been adequately tested or explored.

Future authoring concepts might combine various elements of present ones, such as structured quizzes and unstructured "worlds" of self-discovery, as mentioned in connection with Dr. Bork's work. So far, however, his discovery programs, because of their graphic nature, are difficult to create. As he puts it, "All of us working with CAI are still relative amateurs at learning how to use graphic images effectively in communications. Often the images we have used in the past, representations copied out of the world itself, turn out to be quite inadequate for teaching purposes."

With most (but not all) CAI material, students are reported by both the ETS and CAI instructors to feel the medium gives them more personalized instruction, not less. It allows patient answers to all their questions, and human aid as required. But even CAI proponents wonder what would have happened if all that money (more than $232 million since 1965) spent on programming time and hardware had been invested instead in increasing the amount of time teachers could spend with students without any machinery—and whether, in that case, the course of education would be different today. Eric McWilliams, who heads the NSF's Cognitive Science Department, says, "Educators have got to realize there is no such thing as a free lunch. Only a lot of hard work in a lot of different areas is going to better the educational process." ◆

Sugarman—A second chance for computer-aided instruction